THE WHITE ROAD WESTWARDS

'It's the white road westwards is the road I must tread
To the green grass, the cool grass, and rest for heart and head,
To the violets, and the warm hearts, and the thrushes' song
In the fine land, the west land, the land where I belong.'

JOHN MASEFIELD

The
White Road Westwards

by
'*B B*'

Illustrated by
DENYS WATKINS-PITCHFORD
ARCA FRSA

COLT BOOKS
Cambridge

COLT BOOKS LTD
9 Clarendon Road
Cambridge CB2 2BH
tel 01223 347047   fax 01223 365866

First published by Nicholas Kaye 1961

This edition first published by
Colt Books 2001

ISBN 0 905899 32 6

British Library Cataloguing in Publication Data
A catalogue record for this book is available from the
British Library

Printed and bound in Great Britain by
Biddles Ltd, *www.biddles.co.uk*

Contents

DENYS WATKINS-PITCHFORD, or 'BB' as he is known, was born in 1905. He grew up in Northamptonshire, where he spent many hours out in the open air as ill health prevented him from being sent to boarding school. He studied art in Paris and at The Royal College of Art in London, and for seventeen years was art master at Rugby School. He was already illustrating books before he began to write under his pseudonym, 'BB'.

The Sportsman's Bedside Book (1937) was the first to carry these now famous initials, followed by *Wild Lone, the Story of a Pytchley Fox* (1939) and *Manka, The Sky Gypsy, The Story of a Wild Goose* (1939). He was awarded the Carnegie Medal for *The Little Grey Men* (1941), the tale of the last gnomes in England, which established him in the forefront of literature for children. Many titles followed for both adults and children, and his reputation as a naturalist was further enhanced by contributions to *The Field, Country Life* and *Shooting Times*. He died in 1990.

Illustrations

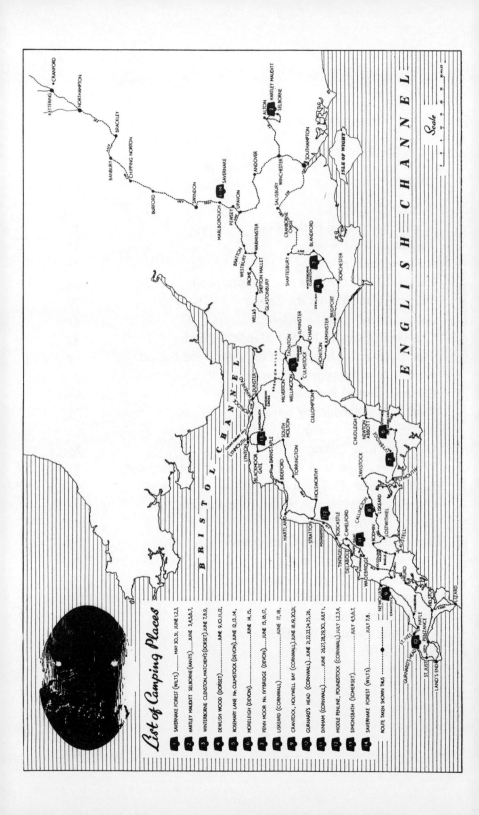

List of Camping Places

1. SAVERNAKE FOREST (WILTS) ...... MAY 30, 31, JUNE 1, 2, 3.
2. HARTLEY MAUDITT SELBORNE (HANTS) ...... JUNE 3, 4, 5, 6, 7.
3. WINTERBORNE CLENSTON, MATCHENS (DORSET) JUNE 7, 8, 9.
4. DEWLISH WOOD (DORSET) ...... JUNE 9, 10, 11, 12.
5. ROSEMARY LANE Nr. CULMSTOCK (DEVON) JUNE 12, 13, 14.
6. MORELEIGH (DEVON) ...... JUNE 14, 15.
7. PENN MOOR Nr. IVYBRIDGE (DEVON) ...... JUNE 15, 16, 17.
8. LISKEARD (CORNWALL) ...... JUNE 17, 18.
9. CRANTOCK, HOLYWELL BAY (CORNWALL) JUNE 18, 19, 20, 21.
10. GURNARD'S HEAD (CORNWALL) ...... JUNE 21, 22, 23, 24, 25, 26.
11. DINHAM (CORNWALL) ...... JUNE 26, 27, 28, 29, 30, JULY 1.
12. MIDDLE PENLINE, POUNDSTOCK (CORNWALL) JULY 1, 2, 3, 4.
13. SIMONSBATH (SOMERSET) ...... JULY 4, 5, 6, 7.
14. SAVERNAKE FOREST (WILTS) ...... JULY 7, 8.

ROUTE TAKEN SHOWN THUS ....

CHAPTER ONE

Badgers' Castle

O N the very crown of the high cliffs west of Gurnard's Head in Cornwall, among the heath, bracken and furze, I discovered a colony of badgers. By the size and intricate ramifications of their tunnels it was obviously of great antiquity. Surely no badgers anywhere in Britain, save perhaps in the Scottish Highlands, have such a romantic castle by the sea!

The massive Atlantic washes their doorstep, its voice must be forever sounding in the complicated system of subterranean passages. No doubt, on nights of violent winter storms, when the mounting combers thud against the foot of these granite cliffs, the sensible animals feel the earth quiver at the impact but are unafraid.

* * *

To reach this secret and remote spot I had to walk through acres of bramble and bracken which, in places, formed almost impenetrable knee-high barriers. I had discovered this sett purely by chance on my rambles about the cliffs, and I determined that I would go and watch for the emergence of these shy, wise creatures. The evening I chose for my expedition was the twenty-fifth of June. It was misty and warm with a faint breeze from the north. It was a long walk from camp over stone walls and along hillsides thick with bracken, so I had to allow an hour to reach the place. I did not reach it until well after eight o'clock, and after studying the direction of the wind, I lay down among the furze and bracken some thirty yards from the nearest hole. It was a good position, from which I could command most of the burrows, whose dark mouths were clearly visible among the bracken.

Badger-watching must be rather like ghost-watching. I had a friend who once spent a night alone at the famous haunted Borley rectory in Suffolk. He told me that once he had begun his vigil the slightest natural noise, the click of a moth, or rustle in the grass, assumed vast importance.

I noted that bumble bees were still labouring at nine o'clock. Two linnets—a female with a young one—came and fed soon after, one on a seeded head of sorrel, the other on a head of thrift.

All over the furze was a mass of tendrils as fine as hair, and of a rusty colour which gave to the heather and furze a burnt appearance, as though it had been ravaged by fire. This was a parasitical growth, the lesser dodder. Earlier in the season it bears a pretty wax-like flower of a pale pink colour. It was abundant at 'Badgers' Castle', and I had noticed it in great profusion at the Lizard, where it made the cliff-top growth quite unsightly.

The sun seemed a long time settling down to the horizon. It appeared to hang motionless, like a pallid shield, in the mists over the sea, and the gentle wind died away to nothing.

At nine-twenty my eye caught a movement to the right of the rampart, by a thick mass of furze.

I raised my glasses and saw (to my surprise) a very old doe rabbit. She fed with her back to me, her pink ears twitching, and finally vanished in a green hollow. At nine-thirty, a half-grown youngster came darting over the left-hand rim of the hollow. It sat a moment nibbling the head of a thrift, then scuttled away out of sight into the fern.

Badger's Castle

I wondered if my scent was being carried that way by some freak of wind. If so, my chances of seeing a badger were poor.

There followed a profound silence, broken only by the faint 'surrush' of the sea and the occasional, curiously muffled boom of a wave breaking on the rocks hundreds of feet below. Some more linnets came dipping and twittering over the furze, quite a musical little band of them, and they all disappeared among the gorse, no doubt settling for the night. A few gulls oared overhead in leisurely fashion, crying mournfully. The sun dissolved away, the loom of the far hills melting at last into a violet dusk. And now, bright and clear, the cheerful intermittent spark of the Cape Cornwall light shone away to the south. I felt very alone in a slightly alien world.

Once I saw something black-and-white under a dark cavern of furze which I could have sworn was the striped head of a badger about to emerge, but when I focused my glasses I saw it was nothing but a tufted block of stone blotched with silvery lichen.

Now, below the cliffs, the sea began to make its voice more audible: occasionally there would come a muffled slam like someone shutting a castle door.

Another late bumble bee appeared. It droned by my left ear and alighted on the head of a flowering thrift a few inches away where it began a patient and diligent search for honey. It laboured with a sort of dedicated purpose, patiently, utterly absorbed in its task. How long would this diminutive scrap continue to work?

Remember, it was now dusk, and the sun had long left the sky. One industrious bumble bee on a lonely Cornish headland, working on until it was too dark for my eyes to see! I found this strangely moving; it seemed it must hold a message, some clue, perhaps, to the unfathomable mysteries of life as we comprehend them, and the meaning of it all. I sensed the struggle of all animate things to *live*.

I lifted my eye and immediately saw that there was something moving beyond the low mound of furze. I focused my glasses, which are especially good for viewing in bad visibility, and saw the top half of a badger's back, which was being violently agitated.

Then I realized that the animal was scratching itself, a habit badgers indulge in on emerging from the sett.

A moment later he moved out on to an open space of sward and I had him in full view, at a distance of less than thirty yards.

There he sat down like a cuddly bear and scratched luxuriously between his forelegs, his blunt, striped muzzle lifted skywards in a grin of delight, reminding me of that delightful drawing by Beatrix Potter in *The Tale of Mr Tod*, where Mr Brock is lying in the bed about to have the water tipped over him.

This done, he sat and looked about him, once gazing directly at me but not appearing to notice me. I have seldom seen a wiser expression on the face of any animal, wild or domestic. He seemed to me to be so *alive* and to be such a vivid creature, full of immense wisdom and cunning, with an enjoyment, too, of his wild free life removed from hateful human kind at whose hands his race has suffered nothing but pain and death.

A few moments later another striped head emerged at the mouth of one of the more distant holes and a half-grown cub came to join its parent. Then, to my huge delight, they began a game of 'tig', rushing around the bushes, 'galumphing' in ungainly fashion, and both uttering strange yelping squeals of delight.

In the middle of their romp the old boar was suddenly brought up short, as though jerked on a lead. He stood a moment with his nose lifted, then, with a curious grunting squeal, he bundled down the sett, followed in a panic by his offspring. No doubt at all that some treacherous luff of evening breeze, puffing waywardly among the heather, had brought him the one dread smell, that of man, his arch enemy.

The stars were lit over the dark sea, the heavy muffled thump of the waves came spasmodically now. There was a sudden chill in my hollow. It was time to go. Those badgers would not emerge again for some hours, possibly not at all. So I replaced my big Naval glasses in their hide case, stretched my cramped limbs, and stole away, taking one of the badgers' own beaten hunting paths which wound cunningly through the harsh bramble thickets and dense bracken jungles.

I hoped I might meet another one setting out for his evening's hunt, and wished so much I could confront him in the narrow way, but not even a rabbit moved. When I reached the stone stile, a typical Cornish stile made of upright slabs, I found a herd of Alderney cows were all lying down on the dew-wet grass on the other side. Their slow heads turned in wondering fashion, and their eyes grew big when they saw my shadowy form pass by, but still their thick mouths moved with a sideways motion as they chewed contentedly, and I could smell their sweet meadow breath.

* * *

As I lay watching those badgers I felt an enormous admiration for their courage and sagacity. For hundreds of years they have lived and died there, died natural deaths for the most part, and were decently interred by their relations, for badgers frequently bury their dead. Their citadel on that lonely headland, shaped like a fortification made by ancient Britons, with its enclosing rampart of mounds and rocks, was perhaps as ancient as that other communal dwelling place, at Chysauster, which I had seen a few hours earlier not far from Zennor.

Chysauster was built before the Romans came, built by rank near-animal men with matted, verminous hair, and skins the colour of old leather, men who smelted the ore among these stony hills, who made their fires and cooked their wild meats, lived, loved and died. Now that ancient village is deserted and open to the sky, but the citadel of the badgers may well be there for as long as time.

* * *

If ever there was a haunted land it is the northern extremity of Cornwall. The trippers do not linger there. They hurry through in the big, vulgar chromium-plated motor coaches. If it is past their lunch-time you may see them, row on row, like fat pale grubs in a comb, their heads lolling sideways oblivious of the passing scene, replete with Cornish pasty and beer. We must be thankful that this is so, that we can have these lonely headlands to ourselves.

You will see in this stony land of sudden sea fogs and bare

rock-strewn hills, strange stone circles and standing stones; some-times rudely chased granite crosses, solitary in the midst of the rough mean fields. Nobody can look upon these relics and be unmoved, for they were erected by early man—many, perhaps, contemporary with Stonehenge.

One can see the strong brown muscles bulging as those primitive men worked under the summer sun, possibly with only a skin of some wild animal about their loins, and the sweat glistening upon them as they worked. If one of them could return, just for a moment, and stand upon the cliff-top in the twilight he would perhaps find nothing changed, save for that mysterious light which gleams with the brightness of the sun from the direction of Cape Cornwall.

There would be the same happy little parties of brown linnets, twittering and twanging about the furze, the same thin crying of the gulls, the same muffled thud of the combers breaking on the rocks. We can visualize this man of the past, bending low in the twilight, examining the badger spoor at the mouth of the sett, and picturing in his hungry primitive mind the smell and taste of cooking badger hams.

Inland the world is changed and changing, men are like locusts, everywhere, but here, where the dark granite of Bolerium fronts the sea with such resolution, there is still to be found the ancient peace, the old security, the changeless things which will remain so, for as long as this old world spins.

* * *

All through the weeks of winter we (my wife Cecily and daughter Angela) had planned, and talked, and argued. Now the actual moment had come for departure it was much as I had pictured in my mind. The perfect May morning, a distant cuckoo shouting in the woods, the sun shining bravely (and how it was to shine in the ensuing weeks, until the rains and grey skies of late July and August made 1960 so dreary), the apple blossom, pink and white in the orchard, the swallows curving over the old barn roof.

I backed Winston, the Landrover, on to the towing ball. Two swallows, lately arrived, regarded the operation from the garage roof. Their journey was over, ours was about to begin.

'Another foot', came Cecily's voice from the rear.

'Another six inches!'

'Three!'

'You're there!'

I jammed on Winston's brake to hold him 'spot on'. The towing ball, glistening with grease, was nicely poised under the cup. A few quick turns of the winding handle and the white hood nestled home with a resounding click.

Then came the usual routine check round: caravan legs all wound home tight, rear-light and warning-light cables connected, all windows shut, cupboards shut, doors locked ... the moment we had been waiting for had come at last!

One last wave to those we must leave behind and I let in the clutch. There is a gritty rustle of gravel under our wheels, Ping, the peke's ears cock as she sits on Cecily's lap, and we move slowly, even majestically, out of harbour.

Before us, in our mind's eye, lie the roads of summer, not the wide main roads with their southbound traffic jams, but the little by-lanes, where the trees cast shadow and the wayside chervil makes a white border, untainted by the shocking weed sprays which make the country smell like a station lavatory; lanes where birds sing, and bright streams glisten under ivied bridges, all of them leading away through the Cotswolds, across the wide downs to Hampshire's muffled hills and Somerset's green heart, on to 'the end of all the land' with its seas of violet green, bold headlands, flowery cliffs and white beaches, a land where summer rules, where, even in midwinter, snows and frosts are rare.

None of us knew where we should first drop anchor; it might be by wood or stream, moor or down. No route was planned, our only fixed goal was the Land's End.

We would go, like a swallow flying south, stopping here and there for a day or two, moving on, a carefree gypsy life.

Come with us!

The Summer Road to the West

Camp in Savernake

CHAPTER TWO

Spring in Savernake Forest

THE green forest of Savernake had never looked more inviting than when we entered it on that late afternoon of the
thirtieth of May. As we passed over the Cotswolds we had noticed
the white hawthorns in the hedges already beginning to rust, but
upon the sides of Postern Hill, and in the forest's heart, they were
at their finest blooming, mounds of soft ivory like the heads of
enormous broccoli.

The whiteness of the blossoms was even more noticeable in
contrast with the brilliant fresh green of the beeches, which
glittered in the heat.

We left the traffic behind us. It was as though we had entered a
vast green room and shut the door. The only sounds were the
'widge, widgering' of the whitethroats, the warbling of the
blackbirds, and the liquid merry bubblings of the blackcaps.
Before us the narrow road was striped with heavy violet shade,
and the westering sun made a radiance on beech, oak, chestnut
and the towers of snowy may.

Before long a green clearing, fringed with bracken, opened on our left, where the new grass of summer was short, a velvet floor, and overhead the soaring beeches formed a fretted canopy. Surely there could not be a more fitting place to make our first camp, surely, in all the days and nights to be, we should never find so delectable a camping place as this?

It might have been the setting for *As You Like It* or *Midsummer Night's Dream*, and due to a 'friend at court' we were free to make our stay there. We appreciated the privilege. I suppose that nowhere in Britain do the beeches grow so tall as in Savernake. Their smoke-grey pillared boles soar to the summer sky, their green ceilings delightfully remote and cool.

I brought Winston to rest under one such mighty tree, and within minutes we had performed the drill, uncoupled, lowered the legs of Heron (our new Willerby van), connected the gas and opened all the windows.

There was a nightingale singing not far off in a wild thicket of seedling oak and beech. So after an excellent supper off the Epicure ham, specially laid on for our trip, I went in search of our musician.

The best song period of the nightingale is mid-May to the first day or so of June, after the males have arrived to stake their territorial claims. Though they are not unduly shy, it is seldom one can actually *see* them singing, for they perform from the thickest cover they can find.

The sun was down when I set out; a vast stillness lay over the forest, no breath of wind stirring even the topmost beech sprays.

I climbed a wire fence and entered a lovely wilderness of young oaks, where the new bracken was sending up its sturdy rods, crowned by their scrolls of green. In places the ash-buff of last year's grasses was still visible; soon all would be hidden by luxuriant growth. From a crumbling oak a tawny owl flew silently, streaked and coloured like an ancient log himself, a true bird of the dead wood, a familiar spirit of the trees.

My nightingale was singing in a small silver birch in the midst of a maze of bushes and tangled honeysuckle. Step by step I edged nearer, trying hard to move silently in the tinder-dry underwood. At last I saw him, five yards away, perched on a spray of birch. He had certainly seen me, but showed no signs of moving; no doubt his wife was sitting close by, tight on her olive eggs, so cosy and warm in their leafy cup.

My appearance seemed to make him sing with greater vigour. He held his head low, not throwing it back as a song thrush does, and when he gave his liquid trill his little throat swelled like that of a bullfrog. He put all he knew into his song. For its size, no bird, save the wren, has so big a voice.

I read only the other day, in a daily newspaper, an article by a townee scribe who regarded all wild bird song as nothing better than the harsh squeakings made by a finger rubbed upon a pane of glass. That writer will therefore have no qualms about the disastrous, and truly magic, mortality amongst our wild singing birds, which is increasing every year due to the use of chemical sprays.

It made a startling contrast to come to this green place from the Midlands, where so many of our birds, all of the seed-eating varieties, have been wiped out. Chaffinches, larks, greenfinches and goldfinches, are the chief sufferers. On a morning in April 1960 I went round the home woods with a sack and within an hour collected over forty dead birds, mostly pigeons and rooks. The smaller birds fall down into the grass and underwood and their bodies are not so easily found.

In 1960 the rooks in the rookery close to my house only managed to rear a quarter of their young. The most noticeable thing was the meagre dawn chorus which, in the old days, was such a joy. Usually the woods near my house ring with song but only a remnant sang for me in that sad spring of 1960.

Now people, especially townspeople, may find this hard to believe—they will think I am exaggerating. But what I say is true; in a very short while, unless something is done to stop this fearful spraying, Britain, or at least agricultural England, will be a birdless country.

The grim fact is that many who make a living off the land have no thought or appreciation of wild life, or its preservation. Many

The heart of the forest

farmers I have talked to have welcomed the disappearance of the rooks and pigeons which is, from their point of view, understandable, but they show no remorse for the disappearance of the hedgerow birds.

In America, they are up against the same problem. I quote a passage from an article dealing with this subject:

> 'The current widespread and ever-increasing pesticide programme poses the greatest threat that animal life in North America has ever faced, worse than deforestation, worse than shooting, worse than drainage, drought, or oil pollution, and possibly worse than all these decimating factors combined.'

This was written in May 1960. The Americans, with their usual vigour, are setting about putting things to rights by legislation, but little is happening in this country. Even the so-called big guns in the ornithological world seem apathetic. We make a great fuss about preserving the ospreys in the Highlands (and quite rightly) but all the time, over the agricultural areas, there is this appalling devastation of bird life going on.

But to return to my nightingale in the birch tree. I stood watching and listening to him for a full half-hour. He never moved from his perch nor changed his position; the clear ringing notes were almost deafening.

When he sang the most beautiful of all his notes, the low sweet 'pew pew pew' which begins in a muted way, stealing on the ear with increasing volume, he held his body rigid, leaning forwards and hardly moving his throat.

Standing motionless in the darkening shade, I could hear others singing far away, for the song has considerable carrying power, and one bird answers another, just as blackbirds do.

All the other daytime songsters were tucked up asleep; blackbird and thrush, willow warbler and blackcap, had fallen silent, only these clear voices broke the silence of the summer dusk, and once, the faint call of a late cuckoo, who sings well into the night at that time of year.

*   *   *

The chill of night made me leave at last, and by the time I regained our clearing, the huge trees towered overhead, ebony clouds of leaves. In a space between two topmost beech sprays a slender moon hung like a hunter's horn upon a belt, reminding me of that other ancient hunting horn, which in the eleventh century belonged to Richard Esturmy, one of the staunch guardians of the forest and servant of the king, and which is still intact, the most prized heirloom of the Earls of Cardigan. It is still blown by the reigning earl whenever Royalty visits the forest. Its voice carries as lustily as it did nearly a thousand years ago. When it was blown a few years back to welcome George VI it set the dogs barking a good half-mile away.

Greater Spotted
Woodpecker Savernake—

CHAPTER THREE

Forest Days

THE nightingale was singing at dawn next morning, when I awoke just after three o'clock. I lay listening to these first birds, seeing through the uncurtained window of our little van the solemn misty forest 'vast and lone'. Everything was awaiting the coming of the sun. The first bird to sing was a song thrush, and then the stockdoves began 'grunting', up in the ruined beech boles hard by our camp. A great many of the old beeches in Savernake were pollarded over a hundred years ago, and these have thrown up many arms which are now decaying, wonderful places for the hole-nesting birds such as woodpeckers, owls or redstarts.

By a quarter past four the dawn chorus was well under way. Soon the sun rose in a cloudless sky—it was a most perfect still, summer dawn—and as we sat down at the table, Angela saw a fox cub steal across a ride a short distance away.

We had a royal breakfast, one of the nicest and largest smoked haddocks I have ever savoured! This was one of a number sent to me by a completely unknown friend, a reader of my books who is a trawler owner in South Shields.

By chance he had read a former book (of which this may be said to be the sequel), *The Autumn Road to the Isles*, where I describe a similar caravan journey, taken in the late autumn of 1958 to the Highlands of Scotland.

I had mentioned that we had been unable to obtain any fresh fish at Mallaig, even though they were unloading baskets of plaice and herrings from the boats at the quay. So my kind unknown friend sent us several prime haddocks to enjoy upon our journey, a kind gesture indeed.

Some years ago when I visited Savernake the jackdaws were numerous, but on our first morning I was soon aware that they were much less common. The head forester told me he had noticed the same thing. He assured me that the jackdaw population had decreased enormously during the last four or five years. He gave as the reason the felling of many of the old decayed trees where they nested, but this can hardly be the answer; there must still be thousands of decayed trees in the forest where they could breed. I think it far more likely that they have suffered from the spraying, though it must be admitted that jackdaws are not affected so much by this danger, for they do not forage in the new-sown fields to the same extent as the rooks.

When W. H. Hudson visited Savernake in the early part of this century the jackdaws were abundant and he had much to say about them in his book *Birds and Man* from which I will quote:

> 'An experience I had one day when I was new to the forest and used occasionally to lose myself, gave me some idea of the number of jackdaws breeding in Savernake. During my walk I came to a spot where all round me, and as far as could be seen, the trees were in an advanced state of decay; not only were they hollow and rotten within, but the immense horizontal branches and portions of the trunks were covered with a thick crop of fern, which, mixed with dead grass and moss, gave the dying giants of the forest a strange ragged and

desolate appearance. Here the daws had their most populous settlement.

'As I advanced, the dead twigs and leaves crackling beneath my feet, they rose up everywhere, singly, and in twos and threes, and half-dozens, darting hurriedly away, and disappearing among the trees before me. The alarm note they emit at such times is like their usual yelping call subdued to a short querulous chirp, and this note now sounded before me, and on either hand, at a distance of about one hundred yards, uttered continually by so many birds that their voices mingled into a curious sharp murmur. Tired of walking, I sat down on a root in the shelter of a large oak, and remained there perfectly motionless for about an hour. But the birds never lost their suspicion; all the time the distant subdued tempest of sharp notes went on, occasionally dying down until it nearly ceased, then suddenly rising and spreading again until I was ringed round with the sound. At length the loud sharp invitation, or order to fly, was given and taken up by many birds. Then through the opening among the trees before me, I saw them rise in a dense flock and circle about at a distance, other flocks rose on the right and left hands and joined the first, and finally the whole mass came slowly overhead as if to explore; but when the foremost birds were directly over me the flock divided into two columns, which deployed to the right and left, and at a distance poured again into the trees. There could not have been fewer than two thousand birds in the flock that came over me, and they were probably all building in that part of the forest.'

Hudson was fascinated by Savernake and spent many days there, usually in the spring. I must just quote him once again for he says in *Birds and Man* that when the spring feeling was in his blood, and he felt the urge to wander, it was this beautiful Wiltshire forest which drew him like a magnet:

'At such times I think of all the places where I should like to be, and one is Savernake, and thither in two following seasons I have gone to ramble, day after day, forgetting the world and myself in its endless woods.

'It is not that spring is early there, it is actually later by many days than in the surrounding country. It is flowerless at a time, when, outside the forest on southern banks and by the hedgeside, in coppices, and all sheltered spots, the firstlings of the year are seen—purple and white and yellow. 'The woods, which are composed almost entirely of beech and oak, are leafless. The aspect on a dull cold day is somewhat cheerless. On the other hand, there is that largeness and wildness which accord with the spring mood, and there are signs of the coming change even in the greyest weather. Standing in some green drive or other open space, you see all about you acres on acres, miles on miles, of majestic beeches, and their upper branches and network of terminal twigs, that look at a distance like heavy banked-up clouds, are dusky red and purple with the renewed life surging in them. Above everything we find here that solitariness and absence of human interest now so rare in England.'

Reading this beautiful description of the appearance of the forest in early spring, and especially the closing lines which I have quoted, makes one wonder if indeed Savernake is very different from when Hudson visited it before the first world war.

The forest stands high, which accounted for the lateness of the hawthorn bloom which covered the northern slopes of Postern Hill so that it looked as though a severe snowstorm had whitened the bushes. I noticed a change in the appearance of the famous beeches. Acres of leaves looked as though they had been singed, or cut by severe frost. On examination, they were found to be shrivelled at the edges, and on each leaf was a small white grub. The forester was worried. He told me that for the last two years the trees had been affected in this way, but in the summer of 1960 they were worse than they had ever been. He called it the 'fire blight'. Certainly the appearance of the trees looked as though they had been caught by some monstrous forest fire. When we camped (briefly) in the forest at the conclusion of our trip, this blight had gone, and the beeches had recovered.

Another bird of the forest which I am sure is less common than formerly is the redstart. When I was last there, in 1943, it was perhaps the commonest bird apart from the warbler; every glade seemed to hold a singing pair. This song is peculiarly wild and attractive, resembling in some strange way the song of the wood-lark which also has a haunting quality. Redstarts are solitary little birds, delighting in remote hedgerows and forest clearings. On the whole they seem to shun close proximity to man, though they do, on occasion, build in stone walls. I have always found they are most secretive over the nesting site, which is often difficult to find, especially if it is situated within a wall. But the male bird will work himself into a paroxysm of anxiety should anyone come near, shaking his tail continually, and giving his urgent alarm note 'u-witt! u-witt!'.

He is a handsome fellow, with a vivid white forehead spot, black waistcoat, grey back, and a rusty-red tail which is always on the wag. Birds move their tails to express emotion, which is a fact few people realize. This may be fairly obvious in the case of the peacock but there are other, subtler movements of the tail which are not often seen, such as the tail-twisting action of the cock bullfinch when it wishes to show affection.

My tame bully cock, a very dear friend indeed, which I have reared from the nest, always demonstrates his affection by twisting his tail towards me, *pointing* it at me like a finger.

Why the redstart should be less common now in Savernake is hard to say: I doubt if the spraying has affected them. But I only saw three nesting pairs when I was in the forest. Once in the early morning I watched a fine cock bird with his beak stuffed full of bright green caterpillars hovering round a dead beech, whose tall naked boughs were full of holes and crevices. I watched him for some minutes from behind a tree and saw him enter a hole some ten feet from the ground where his mate was obviously sitting.

* * *

The first of June dawned, as usual, fine and warm, with no sign of a break in the settled hot spell. Whilst Cecily was preparing breakfast she pulled the plug out of the sink. Unbeknown to her, I had by accident removed the rubber drainage pipe which was attached to the bottom of the basin, inside the cupboard, in which

28

A Savernake beech

was stored a variety of eatables and utensils. The result was that all the dirty water drained into the cupboard. For some time there was tension in the air! At such times it is wise for the male to make himself scarce, so as soon as breakfast was over, I went to watch the dead beech where the redstart had its nest. One of the upper dead branches of this tree was perfectly straight with no lateral boughs. It reminded me of a block of flats. Down the years the woodpeckers had drilled their holes down its length, like stops in an organ pipe, and starlings and woodpeckers, and possibly nuthatches too, had their nests there, one below the other.

On the very top of this mast-like dead tree was a small branch which served as a look-out. There was nearly always a bird of some sort perching on it, a starling, or a jackdaw, and once, a greater spotted woodpecker. It was like a rock pinnacle in the sea where cormorants like to sit and dry their wings. Sometimes a starling would alight upon it and sit there singing, wagging his wings with delight. These somewhat vulgar birds have a great zest for living which is a joy to see.

* * *

Not twenty yards from our door was a stout beech bole with a small hole in it some ten feet from the ground. Idly watching this one morning as I lay in bed, with the ladies fast asleep, I saw a nuthatch go inside. When I examined the hole later I discovered the nuthatch had a nest there—the first I had ever found. The cavity had been neatly plastered so as to make the entrance the right size. This is a curious and typical habit of the nuthatch, which bird is extremely common in the forest. The puzzle was, where did it get its plaster? There are very few ponds in Savernake; those that exist are mere leafy cavities of no size. The spring of 1960 was dry, and there were no puddles anywhere near us. Yet the plaster was neatly done and rock hard. The original size of the cavity was quite large, and the area of plaster correspondingly so. It was so hard I could barely chip it with the point of a sharp penknife. This plastering of the nesting hole must take a considerable time and would certainly provide some of our more expert bird photographers with an interesting film sequence which should not be hard to get with the modern telephoto lenses. I do not think it has been done.

There was one other interesting incident during our stay—we saw a fine fallow buck crossing the ride one evening just before dusk. It came bounding gracefully across the track some thirty yards away, and seemed not to notice the white caravan and Landrover tucked under the big beech. It was gone in a moment among the fern, but what a wonderful sight it was to see that shy, lovely creature which moved with such infinite grace.

Some years back I corresponded with Lord Cardigan on the subject of his deer. He told me that there were still a few wild ones at large in the forest but that the Commissioners hunted them down, for they can do considerable damage to the trees.

It is interesting to know that up to the beginning of the fourteenth century the forest covered more than a hundred square miles, and it was unusual in that it was one of the few which remained in the possession of a subject of the king. Lord Cardigan's book, *The Wardens of Savernake*, is a scholarly work packed with interest, and it is, I believe still obtainable. It gives a complete history of Savernake and is well worth reading. Of all the English royal forests and chases (I have seen them all, and wandered in them), Savernake is the most regal.

Surely there can be no more delightful place for the naturalist and bird-lover, who can ramble for the whole of a long summer's day and meet with nobody if he cares to follow the lesser-known ridings and grassy tracks. It is a happy hunting ground for the boys of Marlborough College, who must carry with them, throughout their lives, happy memories of its noble trees and green solitudes.

CHAPTER FOUR

In Cuckoo Grove

OUR wanderings began again on the morning of the third of June.

Brazen was the sun on the Salisbury road, and we thought regretfully of the cool green glades of Savernake we were leaving behind us. Before us was unknown country; where should we find ourselves by evening?

Now I had long promised myself a visit to Selborne, to pay homage to Gilbert White, to see for myself the famous hanger where the goshawk built its nest, and to see the last resting-place of this good old man.

So instead of heading away westwards, we travelled south, by the lush green valleys of Test and Itchen, where crouching anglers stalked the lusty trout. The mayfly was 'up' under the glowing June sun, which shone from a brassy sky; over the water meadows the heat rippled and slow-moving cows, like black-and-white barges, were belly-deep in the meadow flowers.

What better place on a June morning than beside the clear crinkling stream, a rod in your hand and a creel on your back?

But these magnificent trout streams are only for the rich: the humble man must look upon them from afar.

Traffic was beginning to thicken on the main Salisbury road, the road which we had to take for a while before diving into Hampshire's muffled hills. The noise of the passing cars, the dust, the heat, jarred upon us, and we had to travel with the hood of Winston brailed up because of the power of the sun. By devious ways, through Winchester and Alton, we came at last to the Selborne country, with its hop gardens and pinkish-grey earth in the fields, and saw before us the wooded heights above the village.

A mile or so before Selborne itself we stopped at a fine, prosperous-looking farm surrounded by hop fields and flowery meadows where massive cattle grazed contentedly.

Mr Peter Butler, the owner, graciously gave us permission to pitch camp. When we pleaded for a shady place, he piloted us up a narrow lane which led to a tree-girt hilltop. There, in a meadow, was a diminutive church, with a steeple spire, and to the west of it a shady grove of sycamore, copper beech, lime and oak. This we came to know as Cuckoo Grove for a cuckoo called lustily to us on arrival, and later each morning serenaded us from the tallest lime tree, rousing us from sleep. Blue-backed swallows were forever coursing about the grove all through the hours of daylight.

Down in the valley the heat had been insupportable; here, on the high ground, blew a cool, delicious summer breeze—a true hay-harvest wind, which stirred the fresh green leaves of the limes and sycamores and set the tall soft grasses bending. It looked a delectable site indeed, and I blessed our kind host.

We jolted across the field, Heron swaying behind us, to reach at last that welcome shade. There was peace for us here, with no sounds but the rush of the wind in the trees and grasses, and the constant warblings of blackbirds from an old tangled hedge on the fringe of the meadow.

The little lost church of Hartley Mauditt was close by, and the site of an ancient manor house. This must have been of considerable size, judging by the hollows and low ramparts, now overgrown with stinging nettles, where the whitethroats bubbled incessantly their sweet summer song, and wove frail nests of hay. How strange that a great mansion such as this could vanish away so completely, leaving only green mounds and hollows! Did the family die out? Did the plague wipe out the village which once stood nearby, to the north of the church?

All over Britain one finds the remains of lost villages and great houses which, for no apparent reason, have crumbled to dust.

Beyond the church I found a large pond. Cattle were knee-deep along its margin trying to keep cool. Two small boys were fishing from the far bank. I talked to the elder of them, an attractive lad with a freckled face, a Huckleberry Finn type. I asked them what they were fishing for. 'Carp,' he said, and the evening before he had caught eight, all over a pound weight.

He and his friend told me they had stocked the pond themselves, transporting small carp from another pond in a 'cricket bag'. Certainly they had been successful, judging from the numbers I saw moving in the pool, some of them good-sized fish, in the five-pound class, and others busy spawning. I am fond of carp fishing myself. I had of course brought fishing tackle with me, and promised myself a quiet hour when the sun was down.

We had provisions to get before the Whitsun holiday, so, after making camp in cool Cuckoo Grove, we descended the dusty lane once more to the main road and found, in Selborne village, a most obliging butcher, Mr Gallop, who sold us a fat juicy steak, such as I had not seen or tasted for many a long day. Mr Gallop was one of many in Selborne who showed us every courtesy and kindness, unusual in these modern days.

The heat in the main street of Selborne was very great, so after making our various purchases we were thankful to regain Cuckoo Grove and its cool breezes.

Whilst Cecily and Angela went to look at the little church, which was lovingly and beautifully kept, even though it had a summer-season service only once a fortnight, I sat writing in the van with the soft rush of the wind in the grasses, admiring the efforts of a particularly full-voiced blackbird which was singing from a mound of white hawthorn on the fringe of the meadow.

34

Hartley Mauditt from across the carp pond

His roundelays pleased me as much as those of the Savernake nightingale. W. H. Hudson rated the blackbird a finer songster than the nightingale, but I cannot agree with him. The nightingale has more variety in repertoire.

After an excellent supper (of Mr Gallop's steak, and onions) I set off for the carp pond. 'Huckleberry Finn' had landed four fish in my absence, all common all-scaled carp, and the largest weighed one-and-a-half pounds.

Beyond the church and its dark clustering trees the sun sank in a mellow sky, our cuckoo was still calling, and now and again a carp would leap out in the centre of the pond, sending ever-widening rings wheeling outwards. Soon among the distant dark trees the caravan windows lighted up, and the light grew so dim I could not see my float. I left 'Huckleberry' still fishing. I found myself in complete accord with his keenness. Fishing is almost entirely a masculine occupation and here was a boy who fished all day from dawn to dark, and even after sunset was loath to come away.

A few yards from our camp was an ancient mulberry tree which must have stood in the garden of the old manor house. It was full of bloom and loud with bees. The original tree had fallen—its main trunk lay horizontally in the nettles—but from it sprang this one small trunk which still posessed abundant life. No doubt it is good for another half-century.

I could well picture the lady of the manor, one of the de Mauditts, five hundred years ago, gathering fruit from this very tree, and her children playing in its shade on many a summer's evening. Perhaps it was the thoughts of times past which made me wakeful that night and unable to drop asleep, despite the peace of Cuckoo Grove. The trees were black against the sky, and no breeze now moved their leaves above us; the little church stood in the moonlight with the pallid rays shining on the few standing gravestones in the well-tended churchyard.

I thought of the generations of men and women who had passed their lives in this remote spot, when the only means of travel was on horseback; of the inexorable procession of seasons, summer, winter, spring and autumn, up to the time when Gilbert White lived down in the valley below and wrote about the small birds and animals which peopled the woods and fields about the village. For him, too, life must have flowed peacefully, with its hay-time and harvest. He must have listened to the same sweet warblings of the velvet blackbirds from the hawthorns in the 'hollow lanes'. These steep-banked 'hollow lanes', which are such a feature of this part of Hampshire, must have been almost impassable, even to a horse, in the depths of winter.

I will not say there was a sense of sadness and melancholy at this shadowed grove yet, all the time, I felt it heavy with history. From time to time, in the sweet silences of the summer night, mysterious raps smote the roof and sides of our little van. These nocturnal rappings awoke me time and time again, just when I had dozed off. When at last I sank to sleep it was to dream of the people who had lived and moved upon this very plot of ground, the ladies in their medieval costume and steeple hats, the lusty men in doublet and hose with daggers in their belts, and the leather-coated serving men, coming and going.

Selborne Hanger from the hay fields —

CHAPTER FIVE

Lovely Selborne

EVERY able-bodied pilgrim to Selborne climbs the 'zigzag'. This is a winding path which traverses the steep hanger. It was at the top of a lofty beech in this wood that White's honey buzzard built its nest, and the feat of the boy who climbed it has been the admiration of young unbreeched naturalists ever since.

For those who do not know their Gilbert White I give his own account:

'A pair of honey buzzards built their large, shallow nest, composed of twigs, and lined with dead beechen leaves, upon a tall slender beech near the middle of Selborne Hanger in the summer of 1780. In the middle of the month of June a bold boy climbed the tree, though standing on so steep and dizzy a situation, and brought down an egg, the only one in the nest, which had been sat on for some time, and contained the embryo of a young bird. The egg was smaller, and not so round as those of the common buzzard, and was dotted at each end with small red spots, and surrounded in the middle with a broad bloody zone.

Selborne Hanger from the Zigzag

'The hen was shot, and answered exactly to Mr Ray's description of that species; had a black cere; short thick legs; and a long tail. When on the wing this species may be easily distinguished from the common buzzard by its hawk-like appearance, small head, wings not so blunt, and longer tail. This specimen contained in its craw some limbs of frogs and many snails (slugs) without shells. The irises of the eyes of this bird were a beautiful bright yellow colour.'

When we climbed the zigzag on that beautiful June morning and looked down through the chasm of beech trees, with their delicate layers of bright green foliage unrusted by the 'fire blight' and gilded with splashes of sunlight, I thought of that bold boy, one hundred and eighty years ago this very month, climbing the slender tree close by. Maybe that tree still stands, and the bold boy, all that is left of him, lies in the quiet churchyard in the valley below. It must have been a great feat of daring. I imagine he climbed without irons, probably swarming up the smooth slender trunk until he grasped the branches.

*   *   *

It was oppressively hot in the hanger . . . flaming June indeed; but upon those upper slopes a cool breeze was in motion, swaying the graceful skirts of the beeches, and the little winding paths along the hanger-side were dappled with coins of sunlight which filtered through from above.

As I climbed those tortuous paths I thought continuously of White, whose personality is printed indelibly on the village and the woods.

Many who visit Selborne to see his last resting-place think that the tombstone in the church is his, but it is to the elder Gilbert White, his grandfather. In actual fact *the* Gilbert White was never *Vicar* of Selborne. His grandfather was presented with the living in 1681. He died in 1727 when Gilbert was seven years old.

Gilbert White was born at Selborne on 18 July 1720, and he died in 1793. He matriculated at Oriel College at the age of nineteen, and was elected to a Fellowship in 1744. He retired to

A June morning in the hanger

Selborne in the capacity of a private gentleman in the year 1755.

It is strange to learn that before settling in this out-of-the-world village he was, for a time, a gentleman farmer near Ely in the fens. Surely, no greater contrast could be found than between those flat lands around the Wash and these bosky Hampshire hills. He also had a living at Moreton Pinkney in Northamptonshire, as was the custom in those times, but it is doubtful if he ever officiated there.

His grave is difficult to find. It is north of the church, hidden among long grass in the badly neglected churchyard. It amazed me to find that no care had been taken of his grave. Hundreds, nay thousands, must visit Selborne each year because of him. His *Natural History of Selborne* is known the world over, and has even been printed in Japanese. You may see a copy of this Japanese edition in the Gilbert White museum in the village, where I was delighted to find so many relics of this gentle old man, and also many of the original drawings in pen and pencil by E. H. New, who illustrated an edition for the Bodley Head which has long been my delight.

I always find it rather difficult to say why his writings should be so universally beloved, especially as they are in the form of letters to his friends. Perhaps it is because he was writing on a subject which, up to that time, had been quite ignored. Many of his statements are incorrect, but he is sound enough when reporting on what he himself has observed. Perhaps the chief underlying charm about the letters is the sense of serenity and gentle peace they convey which, in these troublesome days, is even more precious; they are the chronicles of a man who had the leisure, the industry (and one might add, the money, for he had a private fortune) to record the trivial happenings of nature as he witnessed them day by day. In the museum you may see his chair and stool, and many documents and letters signed in his own hand; a most obliging custodian will show you round.

We inspected the ancient yew in the churchyard which Hudson writes about in his *Hampshire Days* and the single grave in its shadow. As far as I know, it was Hudson who ferreted out the story of this burial and why it took place beneath the yew.

Hudson actually talked with an old Selborne woman who remembered Gilbert White, which shows how relatively short is the time which has elapsed since his death.

It was she who told him this story.

The grave is of a man named Newland who had acted as hornblower to the Selborne Mob, when the villagers were starving. Blowing on his horn he had assembled them and led them to an attack on the 'poor house'. The soldiery arrived and took them prisoner, but the hornblower escaped and hid for a considerable time in the hanger, only emerging at night when he went down to the village to obtain food. On one of these nightly excursions he was arrested and sent to Winchester prison. He was, however, later released, and returned to the village, where he died. His relations were anxious that he should be buried in a prominent place and prevailed on the then Vicar of Selborne, a Mr Parsons, to allow him to be buried by the yew. This was done. It was only by chance, and by his dogged persistence in tracing the relatives, that Hudson managed to get this story; but for him nobody would know the history of that lonely grave.

— Wonder what's for supper?

CHAPTER SIX

Hartley Mauditt

WE returned to Cuckoo Grove by way of the wild and
lovely Woolmer Forest, and there I spied a large black
pond, set among birch scrub and heath wherein I was told a man
had caught a twenty-pound carp the Sunday before, when fishing
in the early morning. This pond must be the one described by
Gilbert White as Bean's Pond near Oakhanger. The fringes of it
were carpeted with an attractive pond weed I had not seen before.
It had a small blue flower, resembling a water forget-me-not,
but its foliage was dense and of a neat pattern, not unlike that of
a diminutive bog bean. As the day wore on the heat became more
oppressive. Even on our hilltop at Hartley Mauditt the cool wind
ceased to move. It was too hot to do anything but lie on our bunks
and read. Naturally I took up my Gilbert White. By chance I
came upon the following entry:

'On June 5 1784, the thermometer in the morning being 64,
and at noon 70, and the wind North, I observed a blue mist,
smelling strongly of sulphur, hanging along our sloping
woods and seeming to indicate thunder at hand. I was called

in about two in the afternoon and so missed seeing the gathering of the clouds, in the north, which they who were abroad, assured me had something uncommon in their appearance. At about a quarter after two, the storm began in the parish of Hartley Mauditt, moving slowly from north to south, from thence it came over Norton farm and so to Grange farm, both in this parish. It began with vast drops of rain which were soon succeeded by round hail, and then by convex pieces of ice, which measured three inches in girth. In the parish of Hartley Mauditt it did some damage to one farm.'

This storm mentioned by White took place exactly one hundred and seventy-six years before, and as I read those lines the far rumble of thunder reached me, and the sky to the north of our camp grew an ugly brick-red, flanked by black cloud. Though a few drops rapped the grove, the storm passed westwards, melting away in the mysterious manner peculiar to thunder.

*　　*　　*

The late afternoon sun made Heron uncomfortably hot, so we moved the van right into the centre of the grove so that we were shaded on all sides throughout the daylight hours. We berthed the van close beside a large lime tree in whose trunk there was a small crevice within a yard of our back window. In this crevice a pair of blue tits had their nest and were continuously in and out, feeding young. Though our sudden appearance so near at first dismayed them, they soon became accustomed to our presence, and continued feeding as busily as ever.

It was fun to watch the parents at such close quarters. When father and mother arrived at the crevice at the same moment (and this happened frequently) father politely waited whilst his wife went inside. When she emerged she would take the grub or caterpillar from him and go in again, whilst he flew off to get fresh supplies. All the tits feed their young at very short intervals, sometimes every two minutes, and they kept this up all through the daylight hours.

Having nothing else to do I explored the old tangled hedgerow across the heated field. I found it to be a 'hollow lane' in miniature, the ditch some ten feet deep and seven feet wide, the roots of the hawthorns and oaks protruding from the sides, forming a dark, dank burrow. The bottom of the ditch was stony, green with moss, and a very small trickle of water showed there—overflow from the carp pond across the lane. Chaffinches spinked at me from the bushes, and from the thick-leaved oaks numerous pigeons bustled away: they were resting there in the cool shadow, digesting their morning meal. In the ditch I found the remains of a hedgehog; only the skin was left, the inside having been neatly removed, no doubt the work of fox or badger. Seeing these pitiful remains of skin and pale-tipped spines, I was reminded of an unusual story told me a few weeks before by a man in the village at home, a keen and trustworthy naturalist who has lived all his life in the depths of the country.

He told me that one summer's evening he was walking up the side of an old unkempt hedgerow when the hay had been cut. He heard what he took to be the murmuring of rustic lovers from the far side of the hedge. They were conversing in low and affectionate tones. Not liking to eavesdrop, or be labelled as a Peeping Tom, he went on his way until he reached a stile over which he climbed. He glanced back along the hedgeside but was astonished to see nobody there. Greatly mystified, and feeling perhaps a little uncomfortable, he was determined to get at the root of the mystery. So he walked back along the hedge to the spot where he thought he had heard the voices.

On drawing near, sure enough, the murmuring endearments were heard once more, but he was unable to see anyone at all! On peering through the tangle of the hedge he saw two hedgehogs, a male and a female, in the marital act. They were standing up on their back legs, facing each other with their little front arms twined around each other and were talking 'like real people', so my informant told me.

*　*　*

The evening sun on Hartley Mauditt Church

W. H. Hudson visited Hartley Mauditt for he describes it in *Hampshire Days*. I could well imagine his tall tweed-clad figure walking up the path to the little church in the hot sunshine of those far-off summers in the early part of the century, his dark, hawk-like eyes noting the grove of trees where we were now encamped, hearing perhaps the rich warblings of the blackbird singing from the same hawthorn hedge across the golden meadow, hearing, too, the goldfinches, twittering their loud liquid song from the lime trees in the grove, just as they sang for us.

On the sixth of June the weather was a little cooler. We awoke to see soft grey skies which were strangely restful after the continuous glare of the past few days.

We walked again, for the last time, along the 'hollow lanes' about Selborne, we visited the hanger where the silver hay lay in swathes at its foot, making sweet fragrance in the air. We found it hard to drag ourselves away from this quiet green country, which looked so gay and bright in its bridal dress of high summer. But on the morrow we must be on our way, for we had many miles to go, and many adventures lay before us.

It seemed a fitting moment to pay our last visit to the little church, and after supper that evening, I read in the porch some lines by the vicar, which I give here.

'To The Wayfarer

Here is a place where prayers are said
Or, if you'd rather sit instead, pray do!
And as you sit, and think, and rest,
Your further journey shall be blest
For by the King of Kings
You shall lose all pain and fear,
In quietness God is very near.'

I hoped, too, that *our* further journey would be blest. We had, indeed, found peace and quietness at Cuckoo Grove.

CHAPTER SEVEN

In the Heart of Dorset

A NGELA was awake early next morning, and with unwonted energy she made us tea, which we drank luxuriously in bed. But it was no morning to be indolent. The sun was streaming in through the kitchen window which faced east, making a glitter on the smooth face of the carp pool over the meadow. Suddenly from outside came the coarse shouting of herdsmen, the barking of dogs, the loud bellowing of kine!

Raising myself on my elbow I saw a herd of bullocks being turned into the field and we had no fence around our van. Cattle are sometimes most inquisitive and can do damage to a parked vehicle. Ours was new, paint unblemished! Ping (completely recovered from an indisposition due to greed and heat) leapt about, growling and barking at this invasion of our privacy.

Everyone who, up to that moment, had been as drowsy as bumble bees, was galvanized into life. My poor ladies were in a frantic tizzy for female garments take longer to put on, and to adjust. Nighties flew one way, panties another, and to the sound of popping elastic, I went out to do battle with the herd.

But all this alarm proved to be unfounded. The entire herd careered, rocking wildly, from sight and departed over the rim of the field. Breakfast was quickly over and washed up, and all stowed neatly away.

Soon after ten we pulled away across the meadow to the road. I had to swing sharply through the gateway and quite forgot I had not slackened the rear-light cable from the van to Winston. The result was that I pulled the plug clean off the cable end, as we found when Angela went to shut the gate behind us.

So, in Selborne, on our way to the Winchester road, we stopped at the most efficient garage for it to be repaired.

The light over the hanger was brilliant: a clear blue sky formed a backdrop to the many-tinted trees, against which white piled clouds sailed majestically by.

Soon after we left Selborne on the Tisted road, we had the first drops of rain since we left home, a heavy shower which soon passed away, leaving the countryside smelling sweetly and glistening with drops. It also washed away the accumulation of lime gum deposited on our windscreen at Cuckoo Grove.

We became entangled in the toils of Southampton and its environs. Its villas and streets jarred horribly after the green peace of woods and fields. But at last we shook ourselves free and, towards early afternoon, saw before us on the skyline the dark forbidding belt of Cranborne Chase, a lovely wild forest upon which I had set my heart and which I had never visited.

It was late afternoon by the time we reached it and soon saw upon our right-hand side a wide turn-in and a glimpse of a green and shady glade. I swung the wheel of Winston round and we dived in under the trees, undismayed by a large notice board which read PRIVATE WOODLANDS: RUSHMOOR ESTATE.

We manoeuvred the van under some oaks, tucking it away out of sight of the ride and road. Sallows and hazels formed a screen and we were thankful at last to find ourselves in such a quiet retreat and well hidden from prying eyes.

The wind moved strongly in the tops of the forest, flying shadows came and went, willow warblers sang to us their murmuring songs from the close-crowding thickets.

We wound down the legs of Heron, connected the gas, fed the peke pup, who had now quite recovered her appetite and zest for life, and then put up the beds for a peaceful pre-supper nap. Our journey through Southampton had proved a wearisome business. We found we had done exactly seventy miles from Cuckoo Grove.

I had, however, taken two precautions, possibly because I had a premonition of trouble in store. We had not put up the gas mantles (which are better taken down each time you are on the road), nor had I disconnected Winston. I did not like the look of that notice board, nor did I care for the 'feel' of the place; it was what we came to know as 'keeper ridden'. If you 'caravan' long enough you get a gypsy intuition about these matters!

Our misgivings were soon realized. We had barely settled ourselves on our bunks, preparatory to a short refreshing nap, when Ping began a low growling, and her ears and hackles were up. There came the ominous sound of a motor's engine, which stopped. A door slammed. Then . . . heavy steps!

A thickset man in blue dungarees stood in the doorway regarding us with the expression of a gardener who has seen a rabbit in his cabbage patch, mingling truculence, suspicion and perhaps apprehension. His attitude was reminiscent of an outraged stag beetle.

MAN: 'Have you authority to be here?'

MYSELF: 'None whatever.'

MAN: 'Then you must be off in half-an-hour!'

Of course there was nothing to be done about it, no use in argument. The man was in his rights to turn campers off his master's land. After a word or two he was civil enough, and even sorry he had to ask us to go.

The chase is a game preserve, and the keeper was greatly bothered by campers with dogs, harrying the game, and leaving litter in the rides. But it would have served us better if there had been a notice NO CAMPING, in which case we should have gone elsewhere.

The repacking began; poor Cecily with a grumbling toothache, which had come upon her in the heat of Salisbury. In a sense it was a relief to get out of the chase. There would always be the chance of having to move, perhaps late at night.

So all that golden afternoon we wandered, as aimless as a rudderless ship, turning west by the by-roads towards Blandford and Dorchester. For some reason that drive is impressed strongly on my memory. In the fields the farmers were getting in their hay, a fine crop it was, too, despite the dry spring. Magnificent views opened out to right and left, wooded valleys, rolling hills, the men in the fields working stripped to the waist, their skins a golden brown as though fried in oil.

The shadows grew long across the hay fields and the road ahead, sometimes we swung into the eye of the lowering sun, which made driving all the more tiring, but still we saw no place we felt was right for our night's rest.

Seeing a lady in the flowery garden of a handsome farmhouse Cecily went and begged a pitch for us. We had struck lucky. This kind lady, whose name was Mrs Hooper, told us we were welcome to camp in one of her husband's fields farther along the lane.

So we continued along the tree-shaded road to a thatched cottage, and a garden gay with lupins, with bee butts under an apple tree and a narrow track which led over a bright, clear stream. Close by was a small church of horrible design, built in 1840, which was perhaps the worst period for church architecture. It had a brightly varnished door with a brass handle such as one sees on kitchen doors in old-fashioned houses. When Angela and I explored this monstrosity further we found a memorial tablet made of marble (with plenty of fussy scrollwork) had dropped

The Matchams' Cottage with the great wood behind

clean off the wall and lay face downwards on the shiny tiled floor. I learnt later that it narrowly missed a church cleaner who was working close by at the time. Perhaps one day the church itself will fall and the lovely little valley will be better without it.

By the stream was a level strip of sward where trees abounded. The stream itself was a joy. It ran beside our camp, its banks brilliant with huge exotic mimulus, glowing in the sun as gay as Dutch dandelions.

Hudson regarded the colour of the mimulus as one of the most pure yellow shades in nature, one of the most beautiful colours of all our wild flowers. It is certainly seen at its best beside the clear West Country streams, beloved of the trout and grayling. It is, I believe, quite a foreigner in that it was introduced into this country in the seventeenth century. It has a long flowering period from June to October. Part of its charm is the bold way in which the flowers are borne upon the sturdy branching stalks, and the contrast of the golden-yellow petals splashed with a lip of deep crimson is most exotic and striking, reminding one of an orchid.

Other lush riverside plants grew in profusion; white-headed water parsnips; the elegant dropwort, which formed sturdy grey-green jungles in mid-stream, with the crystal-clear water sliding about its stems.

Goldfinches were twittering happily in the garden of the thatched cottage which had a gun, I noticed, propped against the back door. This suggested the home of a gamekeeper.

The owner of both cottage and gun, I soon discovered, was a Mr Matcham. Actually he was a warrener to the big estate nearby, owned by the Pleydell family. At one end of the cottage over the door of a shed was a row of deer skulls and horns. I found to my delight that this little hamlet where we had found a resting-place was in the heart of the Dorset roe-deer country. I soon made the acquaintance of the keeper who told me that he had lived in the little thatched cottage for thirty-five years.

Matcham was a friendly soul. When we said we would be camping almost in his garden for a day or two he said 'That will be fun.' It was an example of country courtesy which I appreciated.

CHAPTER EIGHT

The Roebuck of the Rides

A T seven o'clock on the evening of the eighth of June I walked over the little bridge where the mimulus were nodding in the stream, swollen with a night of rain.

Matcham was waiting for me by his cottage gate with a pair of binoculars slung on his shoulder. Earlier he had offered to take me into the forest to show me a roe deer. His love for his woods and his deer no townsman could ever comprehend! He shot the deer sometimes—for their own good—but he loved them nevertheless.

In silence we climbed the steep path which led through the moving grass. This was bent and glistening with moisture. We drew near the fringe of the woods which hold some of the best roe heads in England, comparing favourably with the Sussex roe.

Now, in that tranquil evening, the clouds had blown away northwards, and the westering sun shone warm, the air sweet with scents; every bird in the world was singing. I heard the purrings of the turtledoves, the cooings of woodpigeons, and the lighter, more faery music of blackcaps, and rich warblings of blackbirds.

The keeper walked in front. He led me through a little hand gate and took a woodland path which wound in a secretive way between thickets of hazel. Matcham walked like a Redskin, each footstep placed gently and carefully so as not to break a hidden twig, or rustle in the fern. He wore a grey-green coat which matched the woodland well, and his eyes were everywhere, though he never turned his head to right or left with a quick motion, for quick movements are as betraying as sounds.

He reminded me of a hunting panther the way he moved and walked, and I, a natural hunter too, followed his example without conscious effort. The shadowed tunnel before us was splashed here and there with intense vivid gleams of green and yellow light which made spots of brightness where it caught the smooth stems of trees. This light had the mysterious quality of moonlight, shining sometimes on some naked tree trunk far in the forest's depths, or, like a searchlight, on a single delicate frond of bracken.

Sweet woodland scents came and went, neither of us spoke one word, we just moved quietly forward, as silently as the shy roe themselves. Sometimes from among the thick oak leaves, which met in an intricate clerestory overhead, a pigeon would suddenly clatter away, as his sharp golden eye caught a movement on the path below. Once a glorious buzzard swept silently from a dead oak bough, the sunlight shining through his rounded, barred wings.

At a junction of two rides Matcham stopped and pointed with slow-raised arm, to where a large tawny owl sat regarding us.

Whenever we approached one of the junctions in the rides the keeper stopped and leaning gently forwards, he glanced slowly to right and left. For at these junctions, where one can see along the narrow green corridors, one may sometimes surprise a deer.

The sun sank lower, shining magically on pink foxglove spires. The sweet silence of the forest lapped us around, only the clear voices of the birds echoed and re-echoed, and from time to time the clarion call of a cock pheasant, an ugly unbirdlike sound, but one which is inseparable from large woodlands and great estates.

We came upon a clearing where creamy-skinned wattle hurdles, beautifully made, were piled one upon the other. A faint blue reek of woodsmoke hung in the air, for the forestry people were clearing

A roebuck in the depths of the forest

some ground not far away (I wondered if it would scare the deer, but the keeper assured me that they were used to it) and then, from out of the hazels a few yards in front of us, there stepped forth an exquisite sprite of the woods, a delicate being with slender legs, its coat the colour of a red squirrel's, that ancient British woodland colour of fox and deer. The roebuck stopped in its tracks and turned its head, regarding us with eyes which were large and wondering and full of fear, two black liquid pools.

What a truly exquisite creature it was, surely the most beautiful of all our wild woodland creatures!

A moment's pause, which gave me time to focus my glasses, and then it swung round with an infinitely graceful movement and vanished in the screening bushes. For one brief moment a hazel leaf shook and then was still; we heard no sound of the deer making off, all we had was a brief glimpse of the pale powder-puff rump, and it vanished like a wraith!

It was a sight I shall treasure for years to come, as dramatic in its way as my first sight of a wild red deer stag among the peat hags on a Sutherland mountainside.

Later we stopped and looked down one long shadowed corridor where, at the very end, I glimpsed something foxy-brown.

'It's 'is arse!' whispered Matcham, as I focused the glasses. It was a young buck. He had not seen us. He was browsing peacefully, his head and neck hidden in the long grass at the verge of the path. Soon he walked into full view and stood staring at us. We never moved or winked an eye and after regarding us steadfastly for a full two minutes, he went on with his quiet browsing. Then something disturbed him, either some lurking poachers, or maybe he caught our scent. With one bound he was gone. A moment later I heard him bark, a dog-like bark, but hoarse and sharp.

It was dark when we walked back down the hill. We moved freely at last, and talked in natural tones.

'I love these woods,' said Matcham fervently, 'it would kill me to live away from them.'

What lucky fortune had guided me to his cottage in that green valley and the rampart of the forest overlooking his hearth!

CHAPTER NINE

By Dewlish Wood

THERE were two little muddy paw marks on top of our white meat safe when I went to it the following morning. Somebody had been smelling round the perforations in the door, no doubt a rat or even a stoat attracted by the smell of kippers.

It was a cheerful, gay morning, with the jackdaws in the belfry making a great to-do. They were endeavouring to persuade their young to voyage forth into the bright brave world, but without success. They would have to be quick for I knew the keeper had his eye on them.

The little brook, no longer swollen with the recent rains, was purling normally though its forest of mimulus and water parsnip, and diminutive spotted trout darted and zigzagged when my shadow fell upon the clear water. Of the keeper there was no sign. His gun was not beside the door; no doubt he had gone up into the wild woods to his beloved deer.

In his little garden, with its gay rose-coloured lupins, the gold-finches were busy, ferrying to and fro between the apple trees and some distant field elms. Cuckoos called in the distance, and the white plates of the elder bushes made the air heavy with their rankly sweet aroma.

We had promised the farmer we would move on, though I had come to love the place; indeed I was so taken with this part of Dorset that I wanted to find another pitch close by. This we quickly did, without any trouble at all. For, in Mr Frampton of Dewlish, we found another kind friend, who gave us permission to camp in a sequestered meadow with a little hanger above it, and an upland field, thick with furze at our front door, within a dozen miles of Matcham's place.

The keeper came to see us off, bringing with him a little bag of delicious strawberries picked from his garden, a gesture we much appreciated, for they were the first we had tasted that summer. We waved goodbye to him and his wife as they stood by the cottage door, and then a turn in the road hid them from view and they were gone, perhaps for ever.

There was a spaciousness about our new camp at Dewlish. The wood was at our back, its leaves turning briskly in the fresh south wind of afternoon. In the thickets of gorse the rufous-backed linnets were busy about their nests, and in the long grass and nettles on the fringe of the wood, whitethroats bubbled continually. One was busy building its frail basket nest in a clump of stinging nettles not far from the back door of our van. It was putting the finishing touches to it, the lining of horsehair, which is such a favourite material and which must be quite hard to come by these days. It was the cock bird who was building; of the hen I saw or heard no sign. Perhaps the cock always builds the nest. He would slip unobtrusively into his little tuft of nettles and emerge a moment later with a burst of joyous triumphant song.

I climbed to a thicket of gorse on the opposite hill. Huge flints lay around and the layer of turf seemed very thin. At the top was a small quarry surrounded by thick gorse bushes mixed with bramble and wild bryony. Seven or eight linnets were flitting about, 'twanging' and 'twaying' in an anxious manner. I soon found two nests, one with newly-laid eggs, and the other with half-fledged young.

The nest of the linnet is always well constructed, of dried grass and small twigs carefully felted on the inside with sheeps' wool. This warm lining is very necessary. Young linnets suffer much from cold and the nest is almost always well concealed in the thickest part of the gorse, though I once found a nest in a low gooseberry bush. How different from young bullfinches, who can survive cold and wet in a nest which is more like a pigeon's platform in miniature with no lining to speak of! You may often see the eggs shining through the bottom of it. Occasionally one finds a thoroughly well-constructed bullfinch's nest, but not often.

* * *

Each evening we were visited by a bold cock pheasant who emerged from a thicket on the hill and strolled brazenly around the van. I think he resented our presence for now and again he crowed defiance, disdainfully strutting back and forth, with the evening sun shining on his chain-mail surcoat. Maybe one of his wives was sitting in the brambles, though unlike the partridge cock, pheasants have little truck with family life.

At about seven o'clock every morning a hare would appear halfway up the slope of the down. No doubt she spent each night among the succulent clovers and went to bed at this (for her) late hour. If she saw any movement by the van she would melt away into the grass with only one black-and-white tipped ear showing like a signal.

She looked an old beast, and I wondered how many times she had listened to the tumbling sounds of New Year bells echoing across these frozen flinty uplands under the stars. What perils had beset her ever since the moment she was born among the bennets of those sparse and stony hills ? Now she had wisdom and strength, and a great love of life, of the scents on the wind, of the sweet purple clover, the shrilling of crickets, and sough of winds. I hoped that when autumn came, when the leaves went spinning from the hanger on the hill, there would not come that day when the farmer and his friends came up the flinty headland with guns in their hands, ready to fell her as she flew (ears flat at first), her sinewy hind legs pushing her along with the power and agility of a kangaroo.

The next morning as I came rapidly round the corner of the van to collect the meat safe, which had been left on the east side (the day promised heat), I was dealt a terrific blow which sent me to my knees. I had walked full tilt into the corner of the open window of Heron! The blood was trickling down my scalp and I felt absurdly weak and faint. However, a nip of brandy soon revived me. Cecily pronounced that I had a nasty wound on my temple. She swore she could see the ivory billiard-ball whiteness of my skull, that sturdy box of bone which shelters for so short a while the thing that is 'me'.

This cut was two-and-a-half inches long, but a plaster drew the sides together, and despite bullyings to visit a doctor, I decided I was not grievously hurt!

After an hour's rest I recovered sufficiently to go up the hill to the quarry, for I fancied I might see an adder there. I had looked for them in Savernake and was lucky enough to find one, but they are extremely shy creatures and you must stalk them as carefully as you would a trout.

My Savernake adder dwelt in a tangle of briar and rush which covered the remains of one of the old concrete ammunition dumps. It was a sinister place, crowded with young sallows. I saw him coiled on two occasions, half in sunlight, half in shadow, short, thick, a drab stone-colour, boldly patterned with a chocolate zigzag.

I found none in the quarry. No doubt the nesting linnets were relieved, for snakes are very partial to eggs and fledgling young, climbing and coiling through the furze to reach the hidden nurseries.

* * *

Our camp was situated in upland country, surrounded by a ring of flinty downs, but no larks sang for us in a land where once they were so abundant. A large flock of sheep grazed nearby, and I had to rig up our cattle fence, a portable affair of poles and telephone wire, which we carried with us. We only used it twice on our trip.

Camp in Dorset: evening light

That evening the sky was an intense blue, the sunlight quite dazzling, and a brisk wind was bending the meadow grasses. I walked beside one of the upland hedges which I studied with interest. The hedges' roots go deep in walls of flint and turf. Down the years, birds have sown gorse, holly, blackthorn, brambles, some ash trees, and stunted oaks, which are clipped and sculptured by the winds so that they are almost like Japanese diminutive trees.

Into these growths the wild hops have climbed, forming impenetrable thickets of green vines which, even when leafless, must be proof against the winter gales, and form fine cosy refuges for wild benighted birds. The hollies, especially, are close-clipped as if by shears. One wonders how these varnished spiny leaves, whose skins are proof against the wet, can conform so exactly with the rest of the hedge.

I came to a sunny meadow facing west. The evening light shone full upon the hot slope where the earth was parched and cracked. A farmer and his men were harvesting their hay in a distant meadow, with carts drawn by white horses, an old-fashioned scene these days. The men worked stripped to the waist, their bodies walnut-brown.

On this slope, below me, was a little oasis of elder surrounded by a rampart of gorse. I puzzled why it should be there, and then remembered the long-lost rabbits which, five years ago, must have had a considerable warren at this spot.

You will find elder wherever rabbits have their holes. The explanation is that birds, having eaten the elder berries in autumn, sow these seeds, which fall down into the burrows and so find root.

This little grove gave me welcome shade after my hot walk. The ground beneath the fleshy trees was worn bare by the trampling of cattle who must have sought refuge here from the sun's rays a few weeks before. Their dried platters showed where they had stood, fearful of the gadfly. A family party of goldfinches came into the leaves overhead and never saw me. The young had striped breasts, like young greenfinches, and of course no gay red upon the head. But they showed the same bright yellow 'wing spokes' and all the time kept up a continual liquid twitter.

BY DEWLISH WOOD

It was a pleasant walk I had that evening, watching the shadows grow longer and longer, stealing forth from bank to bank, and those curious hedgerows upon their stony walls fascinated me, with the continual variation of dense growth. Here, no doubt, upon southern banks in spring, the adders basked; their richly patterned coils faintly stirring at the embrace of the sun they worship, as cosy as cats upon a hearth.

As the sun sank lower I saw upon the far down a great company of rooks and daws gathering there to enjoy the last of the day. Through my powerful glasses I saw they were not feeding; each bird was basking with raised crest. A great many were young birds, all had full bellies. They reminded me of another scene I had witnessed in the North of Scotland, one brilliant January day the year before. Upon just such another steep hill, where the sun had melted the snow from the grass, a great company of wild pink-footed geese were resting, many of them sitting down, some even asleep, enjoying the sensation of gentle warmth.

I suppose that most wild creatures like to bask. One often sees blackbirds and thrushes sitting on the lawn, heads cocked and bills agape, appearing quite distressed as they stare into the very eye of the sun. Apparently they can do this without harming their sight, and you can approach very close at such times, for they seem to be in an hypnotic trance.

The shadows from Dewlish Wood crept up the slope and the concourse of rooks broke up and dispersed, all flying away in a scattered mass over the down. Yet one little group, I noticed, still remained, as though reluctant to leave until the very last minute. High above them in the same field a great red bull with a white face was enjoying a siesta. He reminded me of some fine piece of sculpture, resting there with his knees bent, and his blunt mouth working methodically with a sideways motion as he chewed the cud.

His cows were spread around him but he remained aloof, like a Sultan, staring disdainfully into the sunset.

*　　*　　*

65

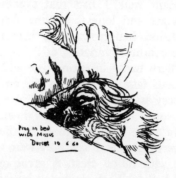

My cut having healed, we went the next day to see the Giant of Cerne Abbas. We tried to get a close view by going up a narrow lane but the smell of silage drove us back. We had a better view from the Yeovil road and I managed to get a picture of it with a herd of contented cud-chewing cows in the foreground.

The origin of this strange image is unknown. It is vastly ancient and impressive. It is wonderful, too, that it has been preserved in its unexpurgated form down the centuries, especially during the Puritan and Victorian times.

One can imagine the horse-drawn carriages passing along the Yeovil road on faraway Victorian summer afternoons, when the local gentry were 'paying calls' upon their neighbours, the discreetly tilted parasols hiding the pink blushes of the maidens and the coachman with a sly grin on his face.

The Giant is the sort of nightmarish figure one sees in modern art. The small, knob-like head reminds one of a Henry Moore sculpture, and the arms are flung loosely in a baboon-like manner.

From Cerne Abbas we took the Yeovil road, turning off it before we reached that town as I wanted to visit the little village of Ryme Intrinsica which Hudson describes in his *Hampshire Days*.

I expected a picturesque hamlet set in a leafy country: Hudson called it 'a charming little village'; but I doubt if he would think it so today. As with many of these out-of-the-way Dorset hamlets, ugly modern villas and jerrybuilt bungalows have sprung up, side

West Bay: the mounting wave

by side with the old thatched cottages. The latter are delightful to look at, with their small windows and sparrow-holed roofs, but not so comfortable to live in, more's the pity.

Hudson speaks of the 'small yew trees' on either side of the church path, where he watched numerous goldfinches busy with their broods. Fifty years older now than when he saw them, these trees are well grown, all Irish yews, and neatly tended.

I thought of the slow succession of the seasons passing over that little churchyard and its yews. How many times have the goldfinches sung since that afternoon when Hudson walked up that path, and gossiped with the villagers who lived in the cottage opposite? And I suppose those Irish yews may well have before them another five centuries or more of sun and wind, unless man, by his folly, lays waste the earth.

But alas! There were no goldfinches to whistle to me on that afternoon, nor were they singing in the trees which bounded the north side of the church. The graves were neatly trimmed, far better than those in Selborne churchyard, and I should have had a look at the church, but I was disappointed in the village (one with such a name should be another Bibury) so I came away.

* * *

We had a look at Bridport and West Bay, and liked the old-fashioned air of the latter place, the busy little harbour, the long beach under the pale cliffs. A dun-coloured sea with large rollers was humping against the narrow harbour entrance. The scene was very French, like a Parks Bonnington water-colour. A group of men and boys clustered on the lip of the wooden piles at the entrance, their gay jerseys making a rare colour note against the biscuit tones of cliff, beach and soft grey sky. The effect of a French painting was heightened by a group of nuns, in black habits, who were standing on the slippery weedy rocks along the beach supervising a crowd of small boys. They reminded me of anxious sheepdogs guarding a troublesome flock. Their black skirts billowed in the wind and the white starched coifs matched the whiteness of the screaming, wheeling gulls.

The peke pup was overjoyed to find herself on the shore and charged about at breakneck speed, dragon mouth agape with glee and ears blown inside out. I think most dogs who are landlubbers are fascinated by the sound and smell of the sea—it goes to their heads. And always there are other beach dogs about, some ill-mannered, but all enjoying themselves.

On the way back to camp we plunged into a maze of narrow roads. Somewhere in the vicinity of Toller Porcorum we noticed that villagers were clustering at their doors and peering excitedly over walls as though expecting to see some unusual sight. Soon we knew the reason. There swept round the corner a vintage single-cylinder De Dion, its brasswork gleaming and its wheel spokes twinkling, with two young fellows in deerstalker hats at the helm.

Apparently we had become entangled in a Vintage Car Rally, and soon we had ancient vehicles panting both before and behind us. Some of the hills we climbed necessitated changing down with Winston, and I was amazed to see how those old cars, fifty or sixty years of age, managed to tackle them. They emitted clouds of blue vapour and made much noise, thumping and roaring, but they got to the top.

The main object of our journey was to find another camping site, but we saw nothing that took our fancy, and when we set out on the following morning we had no idea where we should be by evening.

We said goodbye to Dewlish Wood, its breezy uplands, its gorse and tangled hedges, which fascinated me so much, and soon after eight o'clock we pulled away over the grass to the narrow lane, wanderers once more.

YEW TREE —
CUIMNSTOCK TOWER —

CHAPTER TEN

Somerset Days

WE had taken the precaution the night before of coupling up to Winston, for the sky looked dark and full of rain; indeed, the rain awoke me once in the small hours. I thought we were in for a wet trek on the morrow, but there was no rain falling when we pulled out on to the road next morning. Somewhere in a maze of green lanes at the headwaters of the Culm we came down a steep hill to a farm which lay upon the right of the road.

Here we were welcomed by genial Mr Trim, a John Bull of a man, and of a kind heart withal, for he offered us three sites to choose from; behind his farm; on top of a meadow; or down by the infant Culm which threaded his fields in the valley. We chose the latter pitch for, though the get-in was extremely tricky (with a narrow lane and a narrow gateway to negotiate at right angles), it seemed an ideal spot. And how gay were those low meadows by the brook! A riot of buttercups, campion and pink orchids.

We drew alongside the stream under the hazels, where brilliant new green ferns arched over the chestnut water, full of sherry-coloured lights where the sun caught the spotted shingle on the

A West Country stream

stream bed. The water ran musically from tiny pool to merry stickle, tiny trout fled like dusky darts into the shadow of the alder and hazel roots.

These Somerset valleys (yes, we *were* in Somerset now) are full of alders, that tree which must have its roots in water, and how the thrushes sang as we made our camp! The alders shaded us from the noonday sun, together with the thick foliage of green hazels, whose rounded leaves are my delight.

I recalled another camp in hazels many a mile distant in the lovely valley of Strath Glass, in the Highlands, where, two years before, we had watched squirrels hunting for autumn nuts.

This moist meadow was populous with birds: goldfinches twittered as they did at Matchams', blackcaps sang their bright melodious song from a little thicket a few yards up the brook, and not long after we arrived, a robin came to inspect us, for they appear like gamekeepers to see what you are about on their jealously guarded territories.

Angela went to pick a posy of flowers for our table, ragged robin, orchid, buttercup, foxglove, cuckoo pint, and others we could not name, garnished by little green shield ferns from the streamside.

We went to see Culmstock church that evening, and there saw the famous yew tree growing from the top of the tower. How it finds substance in the stonework is a perpetual wonder. It interested me so much that I later visited the local pub which is always the best place for local lore and information. One old man told me the tree had been on the tower for 'hundreds of years', and he agreed with me that it was probably sown by a bird, though one theory has it that a builder, repairing the tower, sowed the yew tree under the leads. I was told that it is pruned from time to time and a 'hundredweight' of wood is often taken out of it. The roots run under the leads all round the tower. The actual tree grows from a crevice in the stonework just below the battlements.

One autumn day long, long ago, a mistle thrush, perhaps, came and perched on the battlements, and let fall a yew berry which dropped into the crevice. The frail bones of that bird are now less than dust, the tree lives on and gathers life. Well watered by the winter rains, it sprouted and grew and at first nobody took notice of that small green feather of foliage high up on the tower. Somehow it was spared, perhaps the then incumbent realized it was a curiosity and was proud to show it to his friends. It survived the reign of other less interested vicars, and now it can *really* call itself a tree. I am sure that the villagers would be up in arms if anyone had the temerity to suggest it should be removed.

The bells of Culmstock were ringing for service that evening as we walked beside the river which washes the churchyard wall. A fine trouty-looking water it is, with deep holding pools and a merry voice. The inhabitants were trooping into service, all dressed in their Sunday best, and wearing it with that slightly self-conscious and uncomfortable air which most of us experience (especially the male) when dressed for an occasion. Despite earlier sun the sky was overcast, and with an absurd hint of autumn in it. The aspens by the river were rustling uneasily, the clangour of the bells heightened the sense of melancholy.

On our journey to Rosemary Lane, which was where we were encamped, I had seen two amusing things. In the depths of a Somerset lane we had seen a notice, SPRING ONIONS! BABY RABBITS! Whether one was meant to accompany the other I do not know.

The other notice, which somehow had a Tess of the D'Urbervilles flavour about it, was written on a square of cardboard and stuck in a hedge, surrounded by dog roses and honeysuckle. It announced: TO THE WEDDING. We idly followed the direction indicated, through high-banked car-width roads, but saw no wedding and heard no bells, so it may well have taken place some days before.

You will remember that at Cuckoo Grove we had a fine songster in the person of a blackbird (how far away that cool grove seemed now!). At Rosemary Lane, we had a song thrush who delighted us with his evening vespers. He was a fine mimic, the first of his species I had come across to copy the voices of other birds. He imitated the mewing of a buzzard extremely well, and the liquid bubbling call of the curlew, whose voice he had grown up with, so to speak, from hearing it on the furzy commons above the Culm.

73

Each evening he came to a tall slender alder tree within a few yards of us, and always perched on the same branch, outlined against the western sunset sky. On our last evening he sang to us during a torrential downpour which suddenly blew up, and paid no heed to the silver drops.

This same thrush was indeed a friendly soul, for he came to drink boldly among the green shield fern on the margin of the brook, close by the van, cocking his bright eye at us, and showing his finely spotted breast. Once he had one of his children with him, whose plumage showed that saffron tinge of the juvenile.

Here at Rosemary Lane the buzzard's voice was constant, a sound which told me, more than anything else, we were in the West Country and drawing near to the sea. Mr Trim told me that in the thick woods nearby the roe deer were common. This beautiful little deer is much more plentiful in Britain than many suppose. It is curious that it has never been treated with the respect due to its rank as a sporting beast—very different from Germany, where they are strictly watched over with their special seasons. In this country they are regarded as vermin, on a level with, say, the hare, and when they become too numerous, deer shoots are organized by foresters and farmers. They are shot at with 12-bores, often with small shot; many are mutilated and die lingering deaths. It is a pity we have not more influential sportsmen of the calibre of Frank Wallace and Henry Tegner, who accord the roe the honour it deserves.

Returning from Culmstock we lost our way in a maze of lanes. Quite by chance we came suddenly over a hill and saw below us the little white van, tucked up under the alders by the stream.

It was a cosy homecoming: the evening was cheerless and we were even glad to light the stove for a brief hour before sunset. We went to bed early and lay listening to Mozart on our portable radio. As evening deepened the clouds blew away, and over Mr Trim's farm the sky was a pellucid saffron. All the time in our ears was the gentle talk of the stream which formed a curiously restful background to the music.

*　　*　　*

The dawn of the next day was brilliant. I lay in bed looking out of the window at two buzzards which came wheeling over the wooded heights beyond the farm—round and round as though gyrating on invisible strings. The fulmar is a fine glider, but the buzzard 'flies' him close, and they take a similar delight in the sensation of motion. For more than ten minutes they remained in view, sometimes being hidden behind the gay van curtains but reappearing a moment later. There was an up-draught against the wooded heights just there, and they were making the most of it. They tilted at last, mewing faintly, and slid from sight behind the beeches. To a West Countryman a familiar sight enough, but rare to a Midlander.

About fifty years ago, the buzzard was on its way out, due in most part to game preservation. But the first world war gave it a chance—its persecutors killed one another instead. After the war a change came over the great estates, a gradual decline began which has been going on ever since. This change has little good to be said of it, for it means the vanishing of noble parklands and ancient woods. A second world war set this fine bird well upon the road to recovery, and though the advent of myxomatosis set it back, it is still plentiful in the West Country, extending its range even into the West Midlands. Buzzards have a varied diet and will eat grasshoppers, beetles, worms and slugs, or small game.

How quickly does our English summer pass! Now there was no flowery hawthorn, but in its place the delicate pink of the dog roses—and what flower can match those half-opened buds with their rare perfume? And in that second week of June, the uncut meadows were in their full glory, the grass, fresh and green, starred with moon daisies, campion, buttercup, sorrel and orchid.

That last evening I lit a fire beside the brook and its blue smoke spiralled upwards, making a rare incense which remained within our van all night. Our camp at Rosemary Lane had matched up well with our others, it seemed our luck was still holding.

Somewhere, not so far now, summer seas awaited us; soon these secret meadows, muffled in hazel and alder, would be but a memory.

75

Steamers moored in the Dart—

CHAPTER ELEVEN

Devon Days

OUR departure from Rosemary Lane was watched by an
audience of Mr Trim's ladylike cows. We had put up our
cattle fence when we came, but they had never intruded. When
we first arrived they had gathered like school children and gravely
watched us, but as soon as the business of making camp was
completed, they moved away in the most well-behaved fashion,
and had no more to do with us.

Up came the legs of Heron, gas was disconnected and the usual
routine checks were made, and we were ready.

The entry to this field had been tricky, the 'get-out' doubly so,
for we emerged on to the narrow lane to find the wall of Mr Trim's
farmhouse in front of our bumpers and with no room to turn.
There was only one thing to be done—unhitch Winston and turn
Heron by hand! But it was on a steep hill and we had to enlist the
aid of our kind friend who, together with his lusty sons, helped us
turn the van and hold it against the hill whilst we coupled up
once more. On this operation I again forgot to disconnect the
stop-light cable, and we blew a fuse, which scotched our petrol

gauge and trafficators. I had to make good the damage later. With a last wave to our generous hosts we pulled away up the steep valley and journeyed on into the west, with the sun making cool shadow bands upon the road before us.

Midday found us well into Devon, in the neighbourhood of the River Dart, and then began a hair-raising exploration of those narrow steep lanes which lead down to the various creeks of that lovely river. We should never have attempted it with Heron on tow, and were asking for trouble, for the herbage brushed our van on either side. Had we met another car we should have been in difficulties. A guardian angel must keep watch over foolhardy caravanners, for though we spent some hours around midday switchbacking up and down through tunnels of green, with the briars scratching along our flanks, we met no car, no van, and, what was more important, no fellow caravanner engaged on similar rash voyages of exploration! I have not yet worked out in my mind what I would do if I happened to meet another caravan on one of those narrow hills, for backing is a long and tedious process. Another thing, these lanes leading down to the river are so steep that there was literally no flat space where we could find a perch for our outfit. How these almost vertical fields can be cultivated is a mystery, even now, when we have the powerful tractor to pull the plough.

We were told of two possible farms, but at each doorway a snarling cur stood guard, and the inhabitants observed us privately from behind curtained windows, or through the cracks of doors. At a little inn at the head of sultry Tickenhay Creek we were hopeful. The beer was excellent, the patrons friendly, but when we mentioned a camp site, one and all began to make excuses. There was nothing for it but to give up the idea of a creekside camp and to grind our way upwards, boring a passage to the higher ground. Again we met no other vehicle in this breathtaking ascent, with Heron groaning and swaying behind us, her pristine sides being scored again by the angling briers.

Having wasted a good three hours, and some precious gallons of petrol, in this fruitless search, and with tempers frayed, we

77

tackled other farms beside the way, with no success at all. How we longed to meet another Mr Trim! At such times one gets an almost hunted feeling, as though one was an outcast from society.

The shadows were long across the untidy fields when we chanced upon an old roadmender slashing the verge bracken with his hook. Did he, perchance, know any kind farmer who would give us lodging room for the night?

Yes, there was a man 'down the road' who sometimes let caravanners camp in one of his fields. The farmer was out, but his cheerful wife said we might 'pull into a field some three hundred yards down the road', past our old friend with the sickle. The roadmender was delighted and offered to conduct us to this pitch. To our astonishment he leapt upon Winston's bumper as happy as a boy! We rumbled on down the road with the old man clinging to his precarious perch, and found ourselves on the top of a bare hillside which fell away, fold on fold, to pasture and plough, wood and combe, and there, far away, was the misty line of the sea!

How moving was that first distant view of the sea! As a little boy it was always a unique experience to see it from the railway-carriage window at Dawlish; the wonder, the magic of it, was something which cannot be described in words. Something of that wonder still remains with me, though it is but a faint echo of what I felt as a child.

The site was treeless and windy, but the view was impressive. We were more than thankful to find a pitch at last, for we had so far avoided public sites.

How beautiful was that June evening with the long, long shadows stealing over the little fields, the carmine-madder plough-lands, and the numberless thorny bushes which topped the banks. We had the field to ourselves and nobody bothered us. We decided we might have done a lot worse, and probably would do so before our trip was over. I began to realize that unless we were prepared to swallow our pride and harden ourselves to near neighbours, we were going to find private sites very hard indeed to find.

As the sun sank and the shadows stretched longer, the plough-lands turned a wonderfully rare hue of rose-pink. I heard for the first time that glorious elfin voice of a woodlark, singing from across the fields where a little stony bank was full of gaps and crowned with alders.

This beautiful song, which cannot be described in words, has a ventriloquistic quality, like that of the corncrake's 'crake crake' (a sound, alas, no longer heard in England).

I can only describe it thus: U U U U U U U U U U U. A mellow fluting call which carries a considerable distance, like 'a horn of elfland, faintly blowing'. It is a bird I never see in the East Midlands, and I doubt if it is found east of Worcestershire. As dusk fell a snipe began bleating but it was too dark to see him.

Our portable radio forecast rain, spreading from the west, which made me apprehensive of our get-out on the morrow. The gateway by which we had entered was narrow, and even after weeks of sun was miry. But next morning, at least, there was no hint of storm, and we decided to stay where we were for another day whilst the weather held.

After breakfast we left Heron in the field, and boarded the steamer at Totnes, deciding, for once, to be real trippers. We were early so we were able to take front seats, and few people turned up for the sailing, for 'the season' had not yet begun. Whilst we were waiting I was amused to see a party of swans winging their way towards us upriver. They evidently knew, to the minute, when the boat was due to leave, and from long experience, from cygnet days perhaps, they knew there would be idle passengers who would be willing to share their sandwiches with them. So up they came, with a grand thresh, thresh, of wings, and with black paddles hanging down like air brakes.

They had a brisk breeze up their tails and could not turn into the wind, for the river was too narrow. So they landed with a great furrow before them and plenty of spray behind, which drew excited 'Oohs!' and 'Ahs!' from our fellow passengers.

*   *   *

I suppose most people have made the passage of the Dart from Totnes to Dartmouth. It is certainly a delightful way of spending a summer's day. I have done it many times, but never, I think, on a more colourful or lovely morning.

The Sharpham Woods, which were so sorely scarred during the second world war, when thousands of the best trees were felled (and what a task it must have been on those steep slopes), have now grown up once more. Patiently Nature has healed the scars, and the trees, having more elbow room, are as noble as ever. In the summer sunshine of that peerless June morning, with a backdrop curtain of blue sky and tumbled white clouds, they looked supreme indeed. Many herons were in the tree-tops by their nests: fully-fledged young, standing boldly forth among the mass of green oak leaves, their long pale necks weaving like serpents. One old bird passed right across our bows. He held a large eel in his bill which writhed impotently. Under the tide-clipped spreading oaks at the water's edge shelduck swam with their broods of divine ducklings. The black-backed gulls are ever on the watch; that is the reason why the parents kept their young beneath the shielding umbrella of green.

You might think those neatly clipped lower boughs of the Sharpham Woods have been trimmed by artificial means, so exact is the abrupt termination of the foliage. But it is the salt tide that keeps them in check, and gives them such a well-tended air.

We passed the ruins of an old paddle steamer lying in the mud of a creek. I well remembered seeing this same wreck many years ago when I rowed down the Dart from Totnes with my father, one sweltering August afternoon. I was about seven years old at the time. How easy it was to imagine the straw hats, the leg-of-mutton sleeves of the ladies, the striped gay-dog blazers of the men, with their long moustaches, the stiff stand-up collars, the strumming banjoes on those faraway Edwardian summer evenings! Truly, a far more peaceful, less populated, and, I suppose, less exciting world, when people took innocent and childlike pleasure in such river outings.

Ships are a long time a-dying. It is astonishing that these old hulks can withstand for so long the battering of the tides, the constant attrition of wind, sun, and frost. Every day in summer the passing pleasure steamers (descendants of this old hulk) send their wakes thumping and slapping at the timbers. Down in the mud below the keel, fat eels wriggle, and upon the upraised ribs, cormorants, gulls, kingfishers and herons find comfortable vantage points from which to sleep, watch and fish.

There was a string of large, ocean-going cargo boats chained captive, two and two, above Dartmouth. There was no work for them at the moment, so there they remained, prisoners, dreaming of the lift of the Atlantic rollers under their keels once more, and the long, long, thumping tramps across the wide world, beyond the river's mouth. There is much romance about large ships, whether in motion or at rest. Some appeared weatherworn and in need of paint, their hulls stained with bright red rust; one or two, I noticed, were registered at Panama.

Only one, the smartest of the string, a large cargo boat, showed signs of life. Smoke shimmered from her funnel (the others all had their funnels cowled), bilge jetted from her cliff-like side like a mountain burn in spate; men walked briskly about her decks, appearing and disappearing like ants in the galleries of a nest. Some emerged, bearing kit-bags and bundles, none paused to watch our vulgar little pleasure boat pass by nor deigned to acknowledge the waving of handkerchiefs. That cargo boat seemed to me like a restive mare whose harness is being fitted and buckled home. Soon her anchors would let her swing free, she would move stealthily, purposefully for the open sea just round the corner. How glad she would be to leave the hot lifeless air of this wooded river, flanked by its high hills; the horse-flies; the smell of the mud under the June sun! How she would revel in the first great heave of the sea under her belly, and the breezes thrumming in her rigging!

Dartmouth is a most romantic place, full of interest and good shops. Many a Naval officer, serving or retired, must think of it with affection. There is about it all the romance of sea and ships, a romance which is strongest perhaps in those February evenings when the lights of the town shine out across the river, and the flutings of curlews are heard above the Sharpham Woods.

The aged steamers come here to die, but the men who 'go down to the sea in ships' are full of their manhood's pride of strength and health as they learn their trade in the great college on the hill.

I wonder, though, how much longer men will train to be warriors ? Now it seems the destinies of mankind lie in the hands of a few talkative men who may be good and sane, or evil and of unsound mind. Once the Devil shakes the dice there will be no warriors to go to sea, no friends, no enemies. But, sobering thought, the river will still flow, coil on coil, between its steep woods of oak, and the herons will fish in the shallow water, as of old, though no human eye may see them.

Dartmouth's little municipal park at the north end was brilliant with flowers and shady with trees, and I remembered that I had been reading only recently the reminiscences of a commando who sailed from here one summer's night during the last war. The mission was a desperate one. The commandos were to raid a well-defended wireless station on the French coast (this was just after Dunkirk, when Britain, like a sorely-pressed boxer, had retired to her corner to be worked upon by her seconds), and the enterprise was extremely dangerous for all concerned.

The author pictured well the tensions and feelings of those tough men, all in the pride of their youth after months of strenuous training on the wild moors above Fort William.

Death and violence awaited them within a few hours across that narrow darkling sea. For some of them, the castle, looming dark, mysterious at the entrance to the river, and the misty loom of the wooded hills behind, where curlews yodelled, was to be their last sight of England . . . for ever, and ever.

*   *   *

When we returned to camp in the early afternoon, grey clouds were massing, the golden sun had gone. Also, I noticed, the wind was rising. The forecast had been right after all. By three o'clock we had paid our 3s. 6d. for our two nights' lodging, hitched on, and negotiated the narrow gateway without a scratch.

We had not far to go. At Penn Moor we trundled down the delightfully flowery meadow of a 'registered' camp site and found we had no other van within a hundred yards of us. We chose a most private corner under spreading oaks, and from our window could look out on buttercups and bracken and acres of exquisite wild orchids (both butterfly and spotted varieties), and numberless seeded grasses, where portly woodpigeons fed, picking with nervous noddings, their white collars showing above the green blades and red sorrel heads. They were superbly handsome creatures, seen against their summer background of flowers and grasses. Their heads were a rare woodsmoke blue, their large white collars (seen from behind each slender neck) appeared like shields, and the round topaz eyes, the delicate pinkish-grey breasts shading to purest white, made these gentle birds as beautiful, in their way, as the gulls I noticed on the rails of a Dart steamer.

As evening dropped softly about us so did the rain. It whispered gently on the oak leaves and upon the meadow grasses, which soon began to bow under their burden of silver drops. We were glad to have moved from our inhospitable hill with its muddy gateway, which had been slippery, even after several dry weeks.

Later as we lay in bed, Ping tucked up cosily beside us, we heard the rain drumming on the roof with a steady soft tattoo.

*   *   *

On the morning of the sixteenth of June a melancholy sight awaited us. It was as if we had been transported into November. Our world of oaks and flowery meadow was shrouded in a thick clammy fog. Despite this, a cheerful squirrel came and played about among the oak boughs close to the van. It scrambled about among the grey lichens which clothe all these Devon hedgerow trees, flirting its tail over its back, and peering at us with beady suspicious eye. It was a 'grey' but had a strong reddish tinge in its coat, as though it was a cross between the red and grey.

Despite the wintry fog and dripping leaves, the birds were undismayed, and sang lustily from tree to tree, no doubt aware that this was a sea fog, that soon the sun would come again.

And so, all that day it lay upon us in that flowery field at Penn Moor, as heavy as our spirits.

Cornish stile

CHAPTER TWELVE

The Golden Land

WE crossed into Cornwall near midday on the seventeenth of
June. We had, for the moment at least, left behind us the
fog and smell of winter which had seemed so incongruous in a
land of thick leaf, blossom and singing birds. And somewhere
short of Liskeard we came upon a pleasant meadow bounded by
a stream. It was a 'site' like Pennymoor site, which we had just left,
but it was a primitive one; only two other vans were there, which
(luckily for us) had chosen the most dreary part of the field,
away from the brook and close to the millhouse.

Now it was really hot again and with the sun came hordes of
gnats and other insects, amongst which numberless martins and
swallows scythed a ceaseless swathe.

Angela and I, after we had pitched camp, explored the bright
brook which led us away through a tunnel of fern and leafy
boughs, and great green-and-white thickets of dropwort. Small
trout arrowed before us in miniature clouds of sand which were
at once dispersed by the fresh pushing current of the stream.

We visited Looe in the afternoon. The heat was still great; a

Our camp near Liskeard

curious mist lay swooning on the sea. I wanted to explore Looe but every inch was taken, not a space for us anywhere, every car park with FULL notices up, and the narrow streets swaying with people reminding one of crowds at a football match!

We simply had to drive into the town and out again, not stopping for a single moment, shepherded on from policeman to policeman until we were out of the town! This, remember, was June, when the holiday season could not really have begun. We fled away in horror, back to our camp beside the stream.

In Liskeard we purchased six Cornish pasties hot from the oven. They smelled delicious but contained a tasteless mixture of sad potato (slightly blue in colour) and what appeared to be portions of defunct inner tubing. The pastry was like warm flannel. Our Cornish pasties went down the brook to provide food for the fishes.

I know we were unlucky. Later, in a pub in Tintagel, I had some delicious pasties—they really *were* the genuine article, though Cornish pasties are not, I think, equal to their reputation.

Just before the sun sank behind the chimneys of the distant mill, it broke free from a mass of soft grey pearly cloud which lay low upon the western horizon. The level rays, shining horizontally across the moist water meadow, lit the fringe of drooping ferns which hedged the brook beside us. The graceful, delicate, arching fern patterns were gilded with brilliant emerald fire which was reflected, blurred and shifting, in the ripples of the stream. This level shaft of light (similar to that we had seen on another trip, at Rannoch in the Highlands) penetrated into the luxuriant brookside vegetation, lighting up the inmost recesses between the sturdy, lusty stems of dropwort and flag, lighting too, upon the crumbly heads of the elder flowers, and the harsh pink of foxglove spires.

This sudden magic radiance lasted but a few moments, long enough, however, for me to leap from the van and take a picture with my colour camera, as I had done at Rannoch. In the quiet evening, multitudes of swallows came twittering past us, coursing swiftly along the brook, skimming over the yellow flags and the,

The lovely jungle by a Cornish stream

as yet, unflowering rods of rosebay willow herb. The song thrushes sang sweetly, and from the secret nettle jungles whitethroats bubbled.

All at once I was joyful with the knowledge that I was wandering like this through lovely England at the prime of the year, with the sights, smells and sounds of high summer all about us, and with the sense of freedom which was ours. Soon we should be hearing the tumble of the sea upon Cornish rocks and hear the crying of white gulls!

As second by second the myriad sounds of the day dropped silent, so did the voice of the stream grow louder and more insistent. This happy, comforting voice was with us all night through, to make our sleep even more restful.

* * *

There was a strange blight upon the land next morning. Back in the Midlands they were having a heat-wave, but this vapour which hung about the Cornish scene was a sea mist, a phenomenon with which we were to become familiar in the weeks to come.

This, the eighteenth of June, was to prove a day of misadventures and setbacks which were to try our patience to the utmost.

The first came when, having coupled up, and made all ready for the road, we found we could not get along the lane because a man with an ancient car had had a breakdown. He had left it blocking the narrow way and had gone off to find a farmer with a tractor. Nobody could tell us where he had gone, or how long he would be.

The car, which would certainly founder at the most modest road test, was crammed to the roof with boys of all ages, clad in ragged clothes. By enlisting their aid we managed to thrust the ancient vehicle on to the grass, but even so, could only just get by with Heron with two inches to spare.

Somewhere past Bodmin we missed the Newquay road, due to bad map-reading. Quite suddenly a thick fog and drizzling rain came to add to our miseries. We found ourselves wandering in a truly nightmare country of gaunt chapels, grim stone houses, huge china-clay pits, more hideous than anything I have ever seen in the Black Country.

This area might be called the White Country. The china-clay workers, whom we passed in the streets, had white faces, white caps, boots and clothes.

Through gaps in the swirling fog and rain we caught nightmarish glimpses of vitreous green pools which had the appearance of ponds of copper nitrate, whilst all around them the white conical mountains of clay rose up, their tips hidden in the murk. It was like an illustration by Gustav Doré to Dante's *Inferno*.

We spent a wearisome hour trying to by-pass St Austell where we had no business to be at all, and at last won through to the Newquay road after going ten miles out of our way. Six miles short of that town we left Heron in a lay-by and set out to find a pitch. But alas! we were not greeted by any genial Mr Trims. This was an inhospitable land. We were weary with travel and though the fog had lifted and the sun was breaking through, felt despondent. At one place we were offered a pitch on a circular patch of grass. The woman whom we interviewed reminded me of what W. H. Hudson once cleverly described as a 'land tortoise in petticoats'; a slow-moving, dim-witted creature, who did not care whether we stayed or went.

At another farm, where we spied a delightful meadow with buttercups and osiers and old, swallow-haunted barns, we were told the farmer was out, but 'would be back at 1 p.m.'. So we had a scrap lunch in the lay-by, and punctually at 1 p.m. presented ourselves at the farm for the second time. But the man was hedging and evasive, said he could not give permission himself, for he only rented the land and the owner was away for three days. Obviously we were not wanted.

At last we discovered a site near Newquay where trees abounded, and that is something to value in a land where trees are scarce. For I looked forward to the day when the sun shone once more with his old power, and if you are without shade in a caravan you will gently roast like a joint of beef in an oven.

We surveyed this tree-shaded pitch from the site office. There were several tents and vans scattered round the field but, down in one corner, the nicest place of all (to our view) was vacant, so to it we hastened. Cecily soon brewed up some tea and we all felt vastly refreshed, so much so, we decided to take Winston and have a look at Holywell Bay which was quite close.

This wonderful expanse of perfect sand, with its cliff caverns and rumbling creamy sea, made up for all the weariness and irritations of the day. Forgotten now was the ghastly fog-bound wandering around St Austell, with its grimy little villages bearing such absurd (but somehow appropriate) names such as Dobwalls and Bugle. We swam, we 'gyred and gimbled' and the sun shone, the white gulls cried, and in our ears was the continuous rumble-tumble of the rollers.

* * *

If the green glades of Savernake could have served as a setting for *As You Like It*, then the wide sands and caverns of Holywell Bay could have been a perfect backcloth to *The Tempest*. Here are those deep rock pools full of magic (sometimes a little sinister) which are the delight of every child; here are firm sands, miles of them, which could never be crowded, and as we trudged across the hot dunes I was delighted by the numerous wild flowers, those which one so seldom sees, the magnificent horned poppy, the sea holly and many others. Most impressive were the huge trumpets of the sea convolvulus raised sunwards—surely the most striking of all that family.

And now indeed what wonderful days we enjoyed. The sky wore a pinkish look on the horizon with no cloud—not even one as big as a man's hand—visible anywhere in the blue vault over-head.

Massive green rollers came humping in, avalanches of sparkling water, tons of it, breaking in a smother of purest white with boom and thunder.

These spacious sands stretched northwards in a curve and the pattern of the incoming waves, scolloped in continuous lines of

High noon near Holywell Bay

white like the flounces of a petticoat, were the surf-rider's play-ground.

I had brought my board with me and I was soon out in the roar and tumble of the rollers, that rumbling turmoil which fills the ears and is only faintly penetrated by the sharp shrill cries of children and gulls.

Holywell Bay.

I had done some surfing before, but it is an art infinitely more difficult to learn than skating, or even, I think, riding a horse. You must be able to distinguish which wave is suitable, you must hold the board in exactly the right position and at the correct angle, and, most important of all, you must judge the exact moment to launch yourself forwards, just before the wave swings you off your feet.

Eight times out of ten you do the wrong thing and are left floundering, but once in a while you strike it right and swing forwards with a wonderful swift, smooth motion which leaves you, moments later, stranded like a jellyfish far up the sand.

These rare moments when you strike it right make up for all the failures. As you travel shorewards you can look to right and left and see on either hand the rampart of creamy foam, a moving wall, on the crest of which you are delicately balanced like the figurehead on an old sailing ship. Once the surfing 'bug' gets you, it is difficult to stay out of the sea. You may go on and on, having 'just one more run', until your battered shivering body rebels.

Whilst I was thus employed, Cecily and Angela were undressing behind some rocks at the foot of the cliff. There they were surprised by a band of ribald soldiery who emerged suddenly from a cave behind them, just when the ladies had reached a critical stage of disrobing. Attracted by the wolf whistles I saw the whole thing. It is, by the way, of some satisfaction to me that my wife still receives an occasional wolf whistle! This must be inwardly reassuring to a woman, probably it is as much a tonic as a new hat, for when the wolves cease to whistle, you know, in the most delicate way possible, that you are no longer attractive in the eyes of the opposite sex.

Rocks at Holywell Bay

CHAPTER THIRTEEN

The Cliffs and the Sea

WE found the quaint little cove of St Agnes near Perranporth thick with people. They were massed like bluebottles
on meat. This is perhaps an unpleasant comparison for in truth
this chattering animated throng presented a gay picture, every
conceivable colour was there, from black to white, in the wraps
and bathing costumes; all these people were making the most of
the heat-wave and the fact that it was Sunday.

The tide was at the full and they had been driven on to the
small half-moon of sand, rocks and shingle, like a pack of curlew
at high water. Up above, ceaselessly swinging round and round,
the gulls sailed, the sunlight shining through their transparent
splayed flight feathers, and with them an occasional jackdaw.
There was many a jackdaw's nest in the crevice of the towering
cliffs close by. I noticed two of the birds having a mighty battle
at the entrance to a cranny where they obviously had young. They
fought as fiercely as tom-cats and the sand came pouring down
the cliff-face in sudden miniature avalanches.

Few creatures can prey upon these cliff jackdaws and it is easy

94

to understand why they are so numerous. They have always bred in the sea cliffs and are almost sea birds themselves, like the gulls with whom they consort.

I searched those seaward cliffs and crannies with my glasses in the faint hope of spying the sealing-wax-red bill and legs of a chough, a bird I have never seen wild. Strange to say, the only live chough I have seen was in a small cage, in a bird show, and I could not help wondering how it came to be there for the eggs and young of the chough are on the protected list.

* * *

The skylarks were singing early next morning, the twentieth of June, when Angela and I went for a pre-breakfast walk. It was a joy to see them gliding down with outstretched wings, circling lower and lower.

Every creature seemed to be ecstatic that bright morning; white-throats sang from the telegraph wires, their little silver throats blown out like those of bullfrogs; even the gaily painted yellow-hammers, usually somnolent birds like all the bunting family, were lively and in full song, their bright canary-yellow heads vivid against the cloudless blue of the morning sky. In some parts honey-suckle formed the hedge, solid masses of it which perfumed the air.

A polite old Cornishman cycling past doffed his hat with a 'Good morning, ma'am' to Angela, a courtesy one would never find in the industrial Midlands.

Far in the distance the white cones of the china-clay pits were just visible and a ruined chimney or two, relic of the old mining days. There are dangerous pits in this country of ruined banks and golden gorse, fearful chasms which have remained black and silent for many a long year. All round us the horizon was veiled in a whitish glow, sure sign of heat to come. No wonder the birds sang on such a morning!

The dawn chorus outside our van was stronger than any I had heard in early May, at home, and this was now the middle of June, when the 'peak' period is past.

* * *

We attempted to explore Newquay. We had some shopping to do and were charmed with the approach to the town from the south, the ornamental water thronged with ducks, many with babies toiling at their tails, the gay flower-beds, beautifully tended, and the clean look of the place. But at the entrance to the town we soon became trapped in a traffic jam. The pavements were black with people; even at 9.30 a.m. the heat was already sizzling.

After a prolonged wait I spotted by lucky chance that we were opposite the imposing 'drive-in' to a swagger hotel, set back on the right of the road. I could see no future in staying sandwiched where we were for another quarter of an hour, possibly longer, so I put Winston in gear and whisked into the drive and out again in the opposite direction before the startled commissionaire knew what I was about. A brief glimpse in the mirror showed me that many others behind us were following our example, and a line of traffic was beginning to filter past the entrance.

Later I climbed the cliffs above Holywell Bay below the Army Camp on the cliff-top. Why the Government should disfigure these superb cliffs with their ugly shacks I fail to understand. The jumble of hutments is the first thing you see when you come over the hill by Crantock.

To be alone upon these windy cliff-tops, with the perfect summer blue of sea and sky, and with the continual keening of gulls and singing of larks, I found a refreshing experience. Numberless delicate little flowering thrifts, saxifrages, and sedums, grew on

Sea Thrift

Holywell Bay — the rock.—

the bare stony places near the cliff-edge. Some I had never seen before, little minute stars of deep pink, white and yellow.

I have no head for heights. To be suddenly confronted with the most frightful chasm at my feet was rather unnerving. Time and again I would be walking along the gently sloping turf, where the sea pinks nodded in the breeze, and suddenly the turf ended in a vertical drop to the murmuring sea below. And what colours were in that sea! Purples, blues, greens, violets, shading to a honey colour in the shallow water with the shadow of each in-rolling wave traced on the clean sand below.

On Gull Rock the birds were sitting tier on tier upon their nests. It looked as though a heavy hailstorm had rained upon the sloping sides which were white with brooding birds. All the time the echo of their voices came to me across the water, and from below at my feet came the boom and wash of the sea, as it sucked and swirled among its caverns.

Seen from the beach these cliffs at Holywell Bay are not particularly impressive, nor do they seem exceptionally steep. But on top of Penhale Point one has a dramatic sense of awesome height, especially if you look southwards towards St Agnes and Perranporth. On the southernmost rock I stood (albeit with some unease) and the sweep of ocean laid out before me was breathtaking.

The other day I came across the Reverend C. A. John's amusing

97

account of how he was cut off by the tide on the Cornish cliffs when he was hunting for flowers. He tells of his adventure with typical Victorian verbosity, but it may be of interest to quote it:

'On the 24th of August 1831, I happened to be residing in Helston, and having heard a great deal of the beauty of the scenery at Kynance Cove, and of the rare plants which grew on the rocks there, I determined to see for myself whether the accounts which I had heard were true. Accordingly, without companion or guide, I started at eight o'clock in the morning, on what proved to be my perilous expedition. The weather was unpropitious; there was a good deal of wind stirring and rain seemed to be impending. . . . My equipment consisted of a walking stick, a folio book for drying specimens in (which was slung over my back), a packet of sandwiches, and a small flask of brandy. Why I am thus particular in my inventory will appear by-and-by. . . . The first point that I arrived at was the head of a valley, which appeared to answer the description I had received of Kynance, and making my way down with what speed I could, I soon found myself in the cove, as I imagined, though, as I afterwards found, it was in reality Gue Graze, the cove before it. The tide was out, as I expected; I accordingly began at once to explore for Asparagus Island, which, with the imperfect description I had received, I had no difficulty in recognizing in a high detached rock to the right of the cove, the top of which was covered with vegetation. I soon climbed to the summit in search of asparagus, but failed, for the simple reason that it does not grow there. I was, however, well pleased to discover the tree-mallow, which I had never before seen growing wild. A few specimens of this I secured and laid out in my book to dry. All this occupied some time, and on my descent I found that the tide had begun to flow, and that my retreat to the cove was cut off, unless I chose to wade through the water to a depth of about a foot. I quietly took a survey of the cliff, and seeing that it was (as I imagined) easy of ascent, I thought I need not be in a hurry, but might as well rest myself after my eleven mile walk, and discuss my sandwiches. This done, I began to mount the cliff, and at first made a rapid progress, there being plenty of grass as a holdfast for my hands, and of loose stones among which to insert my feet. But when I had ascended some sixty feet, I found myself stopped by a slanting sheet of polished serpentine, on which I could gain no footing, though I made several attempts. I accordingly descended with the intention of making a trial somewhere else, and proceeded yet further to the right. But here I found myself entirely at fault, the sea having come in to the base of the rocks, which were perpendicular. My only alternative was to turn back and regain the cove by wading through the water. I found however, that I had spent so much time in my ineffectual effort to scale the cliff, that the tide had risen considerably, and I could not now attempt to ford a passage without incurring great danger, and reluctantly came to the conclusion that I was in an awkward predicament. The tide had still four hours to flow, so that I should of course be detained ten or eleven hours. . . . As for sitting idle, it was quite out of the question; so, again I climbed the island to explore, but discovered nothing to justify the hope of improving my condition. The only point where there appeared the least probability of the ascent being made by a human being was that which I had tried and found impracticable. I again descended, scrambled over the rocks to right and left as far as the tide would allow me, sat down and endeavoured to compose my mind. Danger there was none, the island being large enough to afford refuge to a hundred men, and I knew very well, from the character of the vegetation on the summit of the rock, that it was never swept by the sea, even in the stormiest weather. An hour and a half I spent in this way, and at last, in spite of all my efforts, had worked myself up into such a pitch of excitement, by picturing to myself the misery of sitting ten or eleven hours in the rain, climbing over the rocks in the dark, and finally groping my way over an unknown country, with whatever vigour of body and mind that I had possessed exhausted, that I resolved to make a fresh attempt where I had before been unsuccessful. . . . I accordingly began the ascent a second time, and in a bolder spirit. When I reached the shelving mass of rock mentioned above I stopped to take breath, and to meditate once more

99

whether the personal inconvenience of spending the night on the spot and the anxious suspense which my absence would occasion my friends, were sufficient to weight against the risk I might incur in persisting in my attempt. I had all but decided on returning, when I observed a small stone in the crack in the rock, which appeared to be loose; this I removed, and thus obtained one footstep, but not being satisfied with my precarious footing, resolved on desisting at once. To my utter horror I found this to be impracticable. The book which I had slung across my back so impeded my movements, that when I attempted to turn, the corner pressed against the cliff and forced me outwards, and had I persisted, would inevitably have precipitated me to the bottom. I could not retain my posture for any length of time, resting as I was on one foot, and being obliged to hold fast with one hand in order to do even that; my only alternative was to proceed, but whither, I knew not. By occasionally making use of my stick to loosen some stones, and to try the strength of others, which frequently peeled off from the rock with a very slight pressure, I contrived to approach within eight or nine feet of the top. Here, however, I found myself in a situation in which few I believe have ever been placed, except in the most terrific dreams. I had gradually quitted that part of the rock which hung over the sloping grass; I had inserted the end of my stick in a crevice, and, being obliged to use both hands in clinging to the rock, I could not draw it out, and if my foot had slipped I should have glided over a few feet of smooth stone, and then fallen seventy or eighty feet, whether into the sea or on to the shore, I could not turn my head to examine. To add to my distress I found my book much in the way; I was supported almost entirely by the muscular strength of my fingers, and a mass of apparently loose stones projected over my head. These I must surmount, but how? The only possible support for my feet was six feet below the summit of the rock, and not more than half an inch wide. I managed with great difficulty to set my foot on this, snatched at, and caught hold of, the top of the rock with the ends of my fingers, and was suspended as it were between heaven and earth directly over the precipice, when the ledge under my feet gave way, or my foot slipped (terror prevented me from observing which), with strength more than natural I clung by my hands alone, I felt a shudder pass through my frame, my blood seemed to stagnate, and a spontaneous agitation of all my nerves in my body commenced, so violent, that this new horror now took possession of me, that the involuntary motion of my hands might loosen my hold. During what appeared to me a long time, but what I dare say was, in reality, less time than my readers take to follow my description, was I in this state, dangling my feet on every side in search of a resting place, and dreading lest the stones to which I clung with my fingers should give way. Feeling that I could hold no longer by my fingers, I made a violent effort, and planted my knee, I know not how, just below my hands; still I was not safe, I was now balanced on my hands and one knee on the edge of a cliff, one leg was still hanging over, idle, and my book, which I had not had the means of getting rid of, had slipped round in front, and inserted itself between my body and the rock. By dint of another effort however, I contrived to throw myself forward, and was safe!'

There can be no softer or more springy surface than these sun-baked heights. All the time, as I walked that lovely morning, I was finding unfamiliar flowers; it was like exploring a foreign land. Some were past their blooming, with strange seed-pods nodding in the breeze, others were in full bloom, yet others in bud. The handsome sea-loving hemlock was impressive, with its cabbage-like leaves, tough and leathery, and its flowers, borne on umbrella-spoke ribs. Here and there, at the very lip of the cliffs, were vivid sheets of bird's foot trefoil, 'eggs and bacon', which seemed to me to be a more close-growing variety than the downland species. Tight cushions of pink thyme, also a miniature form, perfumed the air, and many firmly rooted delicate alpines grew.

I suppose that ten years ago, before myxomatosis swept the land, killing the rabbits in their millions, these cliff-tops were honeycombed with burrows. Some holes still remained in banks and hollows—ruined front doors, half full of blown sand. Perhaps the rabbits will return again, but since they have gone, the plants have spread and flourished, just as the brambles have at home. W. H. Hudson speaks in affectionate terms of the Cornish cliff rabbits and I was glad to see at least one white scut bob into a hole.

These cliff-tops are such a different world to that down in the valley and along the sands, where the holiday-makers flock and play. Nobody seems to want to climb the cliffs to watch the birds, the sea, the flowers. Perhaps we should be grateful that this is so.

Look out with me, look out to the far misty rim of the sea where it meets the sky, melts into it, fused as if a painter has mingled two tones of wet oil paint. It is calm today, only a few instant white gleams show here and there upon its crinkled surface. To the right is the pearly ram of Trevose Head and the peaks and capes of Mawganporth, Towan Head and Newquay.

In the latter place, at this moment, thousands of people mill like ants. They 'swan' around in these seaside towns in an aimless manner, looking at the shops, and at one another. There the cool winds cannot blow; here the pink thrift riffles in the breeze.

Look south, now, to St Agnes Head, and Man and his Man, faint blue separate humps in a silver sea. Now look below at the backs of the ceaselessly gliding gulls, whose joy in life is expressed in flight and not in song, though their musical cries are so much part of the sea itself.

I had watched a large party of gulls earlier, some sixty or so, flocking to bathe in the sweet waters of the stream which enters Holywell Bay over the sands. How they were delighting in the fresh unsalted water. Dipping and flapping their wings, throwing the glittering droplets over their immaculate backs, and sipping the crystal film which swilled over their shell-pink paddles. Sometimes they were seized with a frenzy of well-being, then they rolled and bobbed up and down in delight.

Further up the dunes, in the full eye of the sun, human bodies were crucified on the sand, suffering tortures to win the coveted tan. If people were made to do this as a punishment how awful it would be!

Gurnards Head
from the cliffs

CHAPTER FOURTEEN

'Jim's Inn'

ON the morning of this longest day of the year we were all
packed up and ready to start. Soon after 9 a.m. we pulled out
like a fishing smack putting to sea, with Cecily at the helm, for
the ground was uneven up to the entrance. This site had proved
restful and shady, despite our first misgivings, and we thanked
the warden as we pulled away through the main gate.

The traffic thickened as we joined the Penzance road and by
evil chance we essayed to make the passage of St Ives. I had
forgotten its narrow streets and crooked ways, and soon we were
jam-packed in the usual motionless queue, with the burning
midsummer sun beating full upon us. It must have taken us half-
an-hour to progress five hundred yards. Seizing the opportunity,
we turned up a narrow road on our left and, with a truly thankful
sigh of relief, we were soon clear of the town, journeying on across
sun-scorched moorland.

I heard later an amusing story of the biggest traffic jam ever
in St Ives. Giles, the well-known cartoonist, essayed the passage
of the town with his extra-large trailer caravan. In the narrowest

part the towing gear jammed. It had to be sawn free with a hack saw, and the dammed-up traffic stretched (so legend runs) to Rosewall. It must have been a caravanner's nightmare.

Soon we were travelling over the stony furze-clad hills so typical of South Cornwall. We were now beyond the tree line. All about us were tumbled rocks of all sizes, patchwork fields, and hedges of stone. Spying a lay-by handy to our route we dropped off Heron and went in search of a kind farmer. The first we accosted was friendly and said we could certainly put our van in a meadow behind his farm, but the way was miry and undrained, and the place smelt foully of cows.

At a little wayside inn in the Zennor area I went in for a drink (they had my favourite tipple, Flower's Keg!) and when I asked the landlord if he knew anyone who would give us a pitch for a day or two, he said at once that we could go into his field behind the inn.

This was a pleasant meadow (fronting the sea) which was uncut hay. The view was grand with a wide sweep of cliff and sea before our windows. We were within walking distance of Gurnard's Head and all the grand, rugged headlands between St Ives and Cape Cornwall. We were within easy distance too, of Land's End, which was to be the turning-point of our Summer Road.

How thankful we were to Jim, our kind host, and what a relief it was to turn into that pleasant meadow and park alongside a typical Cornish wall, in which grew twisted and stunted thorn and elder whose branches were trained by the wind, as the Japanese tree artist trains the twigs of his miniature pines, oaks and willows.

By midday we were, so to speak, home and dry, and after a drink in the cosy tap-room, we soon had our outfit ship-shape and in good order.

Winston was uncoupled and run back to the inn yard and after a brief meal Angela and I walked down the cliff path to Gurnard's Head. This huge mass of rock which fronts the sea is a naturalist's paradise. W. H. Hudson knew it and described it, and I had seen it many years before when I went down to Cornwall to illustrate a book for Eyre and Spottiswoode.

'This huge mass of rock which fronts the sea   . . .   '

Cornish dry wall

All before us that golden summer afternoon the sea, limitless and sleeping, lay like a blue rug, riffled here and there by the wind. It appeared incredibly solid from our vantage point, as if cast in metal, the ripples appearing fixed as one sees them from a high-flying plane.

Crickets shrilled continuously in the hot grasses and dense bracken beds, and here and there minute lizards whisked into crannies in the 'wall' stones. Linnets and yellow-hammers abounded, and the happy swallows went coursing by, swallows which had their homes in the ramshackle farm buildings inland. All the farm buildings in the district were roofed with small slates, but these were not, I noticed, coated with cement as they are in some parts of South Wales.

Close to camp, in the hedge, grew an ancient elder tree which fascinated me. It was within a foot or so of our window. Its boughs were nearly horizontal, 'crawling' away from the rude breath of the sea winds, and only the extremities of its twigs dared put forth any leaf. Every twig and branch was furred with silvery-grey and lichen also covered the roofs of the farms and out-buildings attached thereto, all of them a lovely golden colour, due entirely to the growth of the lichen.

To the bearded and venerable branches of the elder beside our van came many sparrows, all cocks, and in full breeding plumage with their neat black bibs, white cheeks and wing coverts of rich chestnut.

I was puzzled for a long time as to why they frequented this tree when they had many roofs and buildings near their nests. Then it suddenly occurred to me that in that part of the world the luxury of actually clasping a twig with their claws must be considerable, for there are no trees whatever. It was their one and only perching tree, which was infinitely more comfortable than furze or bracken, or flat tiles. Speaking of these sparrows reminds me that on the afternoon of our arrival at Jim's Inn I had noticed a pair of house martins busy building a nest just under the southern eaves. They worked with ceaseless industry, and after we had been there a couple of days, had more than half finished the nest.

One morning I heard a great altercation going on, and saw that some wretched sparrows had taken possession and were driving the rightful owners away. The hen bird was flying up to the neat little house with long streamers of untidy straw, whilst the poor little martins wheeled about cursing the intruders, as well they might. These sparrows resembled people we meet on our journey through life who are overbearing, greedy and covetous, who do not hesitate to trample on their weaker brethren.

There is little good in the character of the house sparrows. They are vulgar, dirty in their habits, untidy and drab. Like many undesirable characters, they breed profusely: I have even found fledglings in November. No other British bird indulges in such prolonged and vulgar brawls, which take place anywhere and at any time in street, yard or garden, and they are usually, I suspect, connected with some disagreement over a hen sparrow.

Not many yards from our van was a small concrete storage shed with a tin roof, and to this there came each morning a herring gull.

Herring
Gull

I found later that during the preceding winter Jim, the landlord, had fed this bird. It had come ever since. It was shy enough, however, as are all the herring gulls, and would not take bread thrown to it.

* * *

Humming-bird Hawk moths were busy along the stone hedges next morning. We had seen the sun go down beyond Gurnard's Head like a great red hogshead, now it was up again on the opposite side of the earth, pale, and veiled in slight vapour.

During the night the wind had veered a little to south-east, and filmy clouds were massing over the stony heights behind the inn. A herd of Guernsey cows were in the next meadow, all lying down with eyes half-shut, ears winnowing and their mouths working with a sideways motion like gum-chewing Yankees. The morning was warm enough for adders to be out, which creatures I was told abounded in the district, especially 'down on the head-land'. Jim told me that one was seen only that spring, coiled up under the wooden seat outside the inn where the rustics drank their ale.

As a rule, adders, like grass snakes, are most timid creatures, ready to fly at the slightest sound of man's approach, and they are only too anxious to keep out of our way.

Adder hunting has a certain thrill. You know that what you seek is capable of inflicting terrible pain, and even danger to life, for dogs and sheep are sometimes bitten and die. It is the only wild creature in these islands which is dangerous, a fact which adds a spice of adventure to the search. But alas! though I went down to the headland and trod softly among the cushions of lichen, thyme, moss and bracken, I saw no snake of any sort, not even a harmless grass snake. Lizards there were in plenty, but one had to be quick to see them, for they vanish like fairies.

The day was very hot and the wind had dropped. I lay upon a cushion of thrift by the cliff path, surrounded by nameless yellow flowers. The slope was steep, a faraway late cuckoo was calling, reminding me of Cuckoo Grove of long ago, for indeed it

Sunset at Gurnard's Head

seemed a year since we were at Hartley Mauditt. The summer days were slipping away. I sensed it strongly when I saw the red sorrel heads and the crumbly cream of the elder. Before me stretched the great arc of the deep blue sea, sleeping under the summer sky, with its distant misty capes and promontories.

By and by I saw several Humming-bird Hawk moths coming up the cliff path, or I should say, working their way towards me, methodically searching the yellow flower heads. They were darting from one flower bloom to another with the speed of hover flies, and as they came close, I could clearly see the long coiled proboscis feeling downwards towards the flower's heart, whilst the moth hung suspended above it, its wings a faint mist with the rapid movement. They came, some of them, within a few inches of my eyes, and their diminutive black-and-white sterns somehow suggested the exhaust ports of a jet plane. Soon I noticed that scores of them were all over the hot hillside, all busy with the cliff flowers. Sometimes, too, a handsome silver-spotted fritillary went swiftly by over the hot bracken.

From where I lay I could see, to the south, the grim outline of Carn Galva, rising like a castle above Jim's Inn. Looking at these stony heights and boulder-strewn lower lands one wonders if it could ever be possible to tame and cultivate this part of Cornwall. Even with modern equipment, bulldozers and other plant, I doubt if it could ever be done; the soil itself is sparse and poor. It must ever remain like an untidy builder's yard, and that just about describes the hinterland of this part of Cornwall.

As we were so near Land's End we had, of course, to visit it, for it exerts, I believe, an almost magnetic impulse.

The place, when we reached it in dolorous heat, was seething with trippers. Coaches, cars, mopeds, motor-cycles, bicycles, every known manner of conveyance, were crowded on that last bare promontory of land by the gaunt and ugly hotel.

The summer breeze set the petticoats of the ladies fluttering like signal flags as they stood (a little fearfully) on the high slabs of granite facing the sea. Cameras clicked on all sides, and everyone seemed in gay mood, like people at a country fête on a fine August afternoon. Many were feeling, too, a certain sense of triumph at having at last reached the end of England. Many sported strange headgear, which is a foible with the British when on holiday (but the regular procedure for Americans all the year round). One youth I noticed wore a cardboard policeman's helmet; others sported baseball-type caps of many colours, nearly all the children clutched pink sticks of rock and large spoon-like nameless horrors which they sucked and admired at close quarters. Others carried ice-cream cornets, and into these their pointed pink tongues darted like those of ant-hunting woodpeckers.

Party after party ranged up before a signpost which announced THE LAND'S END and the cameras clicked again. In the car park the bonnets of the cars would have fried an egg, and with every hour more coaches were arriving from which descended stout North Country matrons. They moved with that stiff caution which betrayed some inner tension which could only be relieved within the portals of the waiting hotel. Thither they steered like streams of ants, their gait becoming perhaps a little less stiff as they progressed, exchanging sallies which were invariably greeted with short sharp squeals of piercing laughter.

My interest was however centred on a very handsome snow-white gull who stood with great dignity and disdain upon the top of a large rock within a few feet of the camera-clicking tourists. His pale supercilious eye was fixed upon these extraordinary creatures, and if for a moment they ignored him, he emitted an imperious, peacock-like cry, which immediately had the effect of drawing attention to himself. He was, I saw at once, a practised mendicant. He had found that by thus fearlessly posing for the cameras of the tourists he could keep an eye open for the main chance, a spam sandwich, perhaps, or some such tit-bit. He let me get within six feet of him and I obediently took his picture, with the breeze riffling his snow-white feathers and with the blue background of sea and misty pencil of the Wolf Rock lighthouse in the distance. I had, alas! nothing to give him in payment. Seeing this, he uttered what was obviously a very uncomplimentary remark, and flew away.

We did not tarry long amongst the crowds of noisy tourists but made our way to a more impressive and less frequented cape, the Logan Rock, which lies some six miles to the south of Land's End.

You follow the signposts which say THE LOGAN ROCK and hopefully park your car in a small field, for which privilege you must pay sixpence. You imagine the famous stone is close by but you are soon disillusioned. There is, in fact, a long walk through pleasant Cornish fields where the native mild-eyed Guernsey cows regard you placidly. Eventually you emerge upon a grand, wild cliff-top where gorse and bracken abound, musical with linnets and gulls, and there below you is a fantastic jumble of immense rocks beyond which, towering high above all the others, is the Logan Rock, poised on a tip-top pinnacle.

Only the young and agile can reach the rock itself which is accessible after a considerable feat of mountaineering. White arrows painted on the rocks point the way to the pilgrims, and these I followed until confronted with an arrow painted on a massive slab which seemed to point directly at a vertical wall of rock. I would have climbed this despite my bad head for heights, had not the weather suddenly become sombre, and a fine rain began to fall. Seawards it shut down like a falling safety curtain and the moaning of the fog buoys came and went, a sound which is the most eerie of all man-made noises, not even excepting the moaning of air-raid sirens.

Most people know the story of the Logan Rock but it is worth retelling here.

In 1824 a Doctor Borlase observed (rather rashly as it turned out) that the Logan Rock could not be shifted by any force applied in a mechanical way. The challenge was privately taken up by a certain Lieutenant Goldsmith (nephew of the poet Goldsmith) who commanded a revenue cutter. He landed with a ship's crew and pushed the sixty-ton rock to the shore below. This proved quite an expensive experiment. My Lords of the Admiralty made him replace it at his own expense which ruined him financially. Nevertheless his name survives because of this act of folly which, in a way, is typically British. Every young male of university age seems prone to such exertions. In our own day the efforts of the young gentlemen who removed the Stone of Destiny are recalled, though their names are, happily, not remembered.

In fog and mist we hurried back to Winston and within half-an-hour were back in our van, cosy and snug, aware of the strange transformation from summer to mid-November. Even Jim's Inn across the little grassy meadow was barely visible in the murk. We had, at any rate, reached the 'end of all the land' which was the goal of our journey. Henceforward our wanderings lay north once more. In all our days we had only missed the sun on three or four occasions so we couldn't grumble.

That melancholy sea mist gradually withdrew upwards towards sunset, and I went down to the headland to take some coloured pictures of the evening sky. A herd of curlews was busily flying up the coast in a compact goose-like formation, and the birds skirled wildly as they flew close over the wrinkled surface of the waves. Against the darkling sea a minelayer passed up the coast with port and starboard lights aglow.

I watched it until it was hidden in the dusk.

St Michael's Mount

CHAPTER FIFTEEN

The Lizard and its Coastal Scene

In many ways the Lizard is vastly superior to Land's End. It is not so impressive, there are not the masses of rock formation, it is just a rather untidy cape without even an attractive cove at its foot. But there is no gaunt hotel to dominate the cliff-edge, and there are not the same milling crowds of tourists. We visited it on the twenty-third of June. The magnificent weather had returned.

Trapped in the narrow lanes, with their high banks which led down to the beach, the heat was terrific. Poor elderly holiday-makers were swooning helplessly against the grass banks, mouths open, and with handkerchiefs feebly fanning.

Below the cliff upon which the trippers gaped through the fixed telescope (surely the most profitable racket ever) there was a narrow cleft, a sort of shabby cove, which appeared to be fairly inaccessible, either from above or below. And upon a ledge half-way down, I was surprised to see a pair of kittiwakes had two downy young. These youngsters were, I suppose, about three weeks old, and appeared to be quite well feathered. Both were a soft grey colour which matched the rock ledge well. The mother

Sun-glitter at noon on a Cornish sea

was feeding them daintily, regurgitating small particles which she put carefully on the ledge before her children, as a fishmonger arranges fishes on his slab, allowing them to help themselves.

The father was close by, perched on a pinnacle, obviously feeling no end of a fellow, but he was doing no real work nor helping in any way. From time to time he bowed his head and threw it back, uttering a ringing cry which echoed loudly above the tumult of the waves which were crashing against the rocks below.

The sun was beating mercilessly upon this south-facing rock and the two youngsters were most uncomfortable, shuffling to and fro along the ledge with beaks agape, trying to shelter in the shadow of their mother.

I should imagine that cliff-breeding birds which build upon the exposed ledges facing south must suffer considerably in hot weather. The gulls' nests I saw on the cliffs near Zennor had mostly a northerly aspect where possible.

I do not think that any one of the holiday-makers on the cliff-top at the Lizard noticed these two young kittiwakes just below them—they were so much the colour of the ledges. After a little while, having fed their children, the parent birds flew away over the blue sea, and the poor babies continued to creep up and down the ledge, vainly trying to find some shade, but without success. There was just no cranny which could provide relief, and they would have to suffer the heat torture for some hours yet before the sun passed westwards.

There was a small shop at the top of the cliffs where we parked Winston. Here we watched a man with a wheel working the lovely Cornish serpentine stone, forming it into ash trays, bowls, trinket boxes and suchlike, as well as lighthouses and weather-barometer cases. I bought one of these latter, for the stone was most beautifully marked and clouded with purples, greys, blues, whites and greens. Before the stone is worked it is commonplace and drab, but when polished it is full of rare colour. All this man's work was not catchpenny stuff, but genuine country workmanship.

* * *

The southern side of the Cornish centre rib is not so attractive as the north coast for it lacks the wildness and sense of remoteness. Much of the extremity of Cornwall closely resembles Pembrokeshire. Before we reached the Lizard we passed over that strange desolate and rather grim tract of country known as Goonhilly Downs, once the haunt of rogues and highwaymen. No doubt up to the end of the eighteenth century many a hapless traveller had his throat cut on this uncouth moor.

Leyland called it 'a Wylde Moore, cawled Gunhilly wher ys brood of catyle'. At one time a specially hardy breed of horse was bred there, they were even called 'Goonhillys'. No doubt these horses were similar to the ponies of Dartmoor, rough-coated and sturdy little beasts who could withstand much bad winter weather.

There is a story that during the eighteenth century two robbers dwelt in a rough rude cabin in the midst of Goonhilly Downs. One day they happened to learn that a farmer was returning from Helston with a large sum of money in his pockets, the fruits of bargaining in the market. They planned to waylay him in a lonely part of the track. At the expected time a horseman appeared in the distance and headed their way. Rather hastily the two wretches opened fire on the traveller but missed him, and their would-be victim (who was not the farmer at all) galloped away safe and unharmed.

But shortly afterwards the farmer himself came in sight and they shot him and dragged him from his horse. He was later found and carried to a farmhouse where he died the same night. He said he did not know who his murderers were but that in the struggle his horse had stepped on the foot of one of them. This led to the identification of the murderers who forfeited their lives on the gallows.

Today, Goonhilly Downs are still wrapped in a depressing atmosphere. It is a featureless, stony waste full of scrub willow, dwarf sallow and dotted with ruined buildings left from the last war. We looked at it with a view to a possible camp site but something in the atmosphere turned us against it.

A sea fog shut down again that evening when we returned to

camp, and the wind died away. Far to the south thunder grumbled, the sky grew dark over the sea.

I do not know whether it was the solemn stillness and the complete absence of bird song, but I suddenly sensed that summer had, for us, come to the full tide. It was like that pause one observes in the movement of the oily flood which fills the gutters of the marsh, and the little fish-smelling harbours, that moment when it is poised and motionless before once more retreating on its eternal journey.

I remembered then that we had indeed passed the longest day, and the white hawthorns of Savernake and the cool green glades seemed distant indeed.

As the sun sank the fog thickened until it lay around us like a wall. From time to time the sun appeared, a flat and pallid disc, then it vanished completely away.

At 3 a.m. the barking of farm dogs awakened me, and when I drew aside the van curtain and peered out the fog had gone. The stars were shining, and dawn was stealing up over the barren stony hills to the east of us. A strange grey chill embraced the world; even the sea slept silently in its coves. But at morning the fog came down again thicker than ever; Jim's Inn vanished in the murk.

These summer fogs are common along the north coast at this time of the year. I was reminded of the legend of the Hooper, a ghostly manifestation which occurred from time to time in the eighteenth and nineteenth centuries off Land's End. Apparently this was a mysterious cloud of vapour which came in from the sea, when all else was free from mist. A dull light shone in the heart of it from which came dull whooping and moaning sounds. Bold fishermen (so it was said) who went out to probe the mystery, vanished from human ken never to be seen again!

However, when we come to study these old legends, we find a possible curious explanation for these strange unearthly sights and sounds.

I know an authentic case of a man who was walking at night in a wooded valley in the North of England, many years ago. To his astonishment he heard the noise of a train and saw the lighted carriages shuttling through the trees. There was of course no railway there, but, later, one was built and in that man's lifetime. Maybe the luminous mist, the dull lights, the whooping sounds, were ghostly bell buoys and fog buoys, which later came to be moored at those places. James Dunne, author of *An Experiment with Time*, can give us a perfectly logical explanation of all this, but it is far too complicated to go into here.

When later that day we went over the centre of the land to the south side, we found the fog had entirely vanished, and the sea and hills were glowing in the summer sun. People were bathing at Marazion, and St Michael's Mount was like a fairy castle wrapped in pearly mist and seemingly suspended in mid-air. Soon it was so hot we had to brail up the back of Winston, yet we learnt later that at Jim's Inn the fog had persisted all day, as we found when we returned.

We visited that most attractive and quite famous little cove of Gunwallowe—indeed, who could ever pass by a signpost with such a name upon it? We were greatly taken with it and its queer grey church tucked up under its little cliff close to the beach, over which the waves send their sheets of spray when a westerly gale is blowing.

Old C. A. Johns, who was author of a book on wild flowers which is still a standard work, visited Gunwallowe during his rambles about this coast. He tells the story of the treasure (or rather treasures) of Gunwallowe which are supposed to lie at the foot of the cliff next to the church. The story has been rehashed and quoted in every book on Cornwall. Here I do likewise, and without apology for no mention of this strange and delightful little cove can be made without some reference to its 'treasure'.

Johns says:

'Beyond Gunwallowe church the land rises, and the coast again becomes bold for a short distance. The cliffs, though not lofty, are precipitous, and offer no chance of escape to any unfortunate vessel which may chance to be driven within reach of the rocks.

'About the year 1785, a vessel laden with wool, and having also on board two and a half tons of money, was driven ashore a few hundred yards west of the church, and soon went to pieces. Ever since, at intervals after a storm, dollars have been picked up upon the beach, but never in sufficient numbers to compensate for the time wasted in the search. No measures however, on a large scale, for the recovery of the precious cargo were adopted until three years ago (*Johns was writing* circa *1848*) when people were startled to hear that a party of adventurers were going to sink a "dollar mine" in the sea. The vessel had gone to pieces between two rocks at a short distance from the base of the cliff, and here it was proposed to construct a kind of coffer-dam, from which the water was to be pumped out and the dollars to be picked up at leisure. Mad though the scheme was, operations were actually commenced; a path was cut in the face of the cliff, iron rods were fixed into the rocks, and several beams of timber laid down, when a breeze set in from the south-west, and in the course of a few hours the work of as many weeks was destroyed. The woodwork was ripped up as effectually as if it had been a mere wickerwork cage, and the coast was soon lined with fragments. It is not likely the attempt will be renewed.

'This is not the only unsuccessful search for treasure which has been made at Gunwallowe. In the sand banks near the church (or as others say, at Kynance Cove), the notorious buccaneer, Captain Avery, is reported to have buried several chests of treasure previous to his leaving England on the voyage from which he never returned. So strongly did this opinion prevail that Mr John Knill, a collector of customs at St Ives, procured about the year 1770, a grant of treasure trove and expended some money in fruitless search.'

I could not help wondering, as I looked at the very spot below the cliffs where the treasure is supposed to lie, whether anyone has seriously considered a diving operation with modern gear. The iron stakes driven into the cliffs may still be there and would form a sure pointer to the exact spot where the ship went aground. I commend the idea to any young adventurer. He might have better results than those recently reported by the Duke of Argyll off Tobermory Bay.

Then again, there is somewhere close to Gunwallowe (if not at the same spot) a cargo of the *St Andrew*, a treasure ship of the King of Portugal which came ashore on this coast on a wild January night in 1526.

Her cargo, which is known, consisted of eight thousand cakes of copper, eighteen blocks of silver bullion, silver vessels, plate, precious stones, jewels and brooches of gold, to say nothing of four suits of armour for the King of Portugal and a chest containing £6,000 in coin!

From reading all this one might imagine that the sands within a bow-shot of the church must be cluttered up with the precious stuff! So, you would-be adventurers, with your snorkels, go to it. Even in recent years some wanderer along these sands has come upon a gleaming dollar from the treasure ship, so these must be more than old wives' tales, and as far as I know, no other serious attempts have been made to locate the treasure.

Somehow, seeing Gunwallowe Cove and its squat little church crouching and hunched under the shelter of its treasure cliff, and the big white breakers bursting on the beach hard by and dark thunder clouds beyond, put me in mind of a woodcut or a rich etching.

*　　*　　*

Another strange place we visited was Loe Pool not many miles west of Gunwallowe. This is a large sheet of inland water seven miles in circumference, with steep woody hills enclosing it; viewed from some angles it might well be a stretch of the Dart.

The narrow bank of white sand and shingle which divides it from the sea was covered with all manner of strange little plants and flowers, which no doubt delighted the heart of old C. A. Johns when he wandered there in the last century. The water must be fairly brackish. Our peke pup refused to drink it, though she was thirsty, but cattle were doing so, I noticed, on the far shore, and in the shallows many fresh-water plants grew in profusion, together with clumps of reed. Perhaps it is about as brackish as is Slapton in Devon.

There are all sorts of old legends connected with this water. On a grim December night in 1807, three days after Christmas Day, the frigate *Anson*, a ship of the line, mounting forty-four guns, was run aground on Loe Bar in a last desperate attempt to save the lives of her crew. One hundred men were lost in the short strip of breakers.

An eye-witness of the tragedy was one Henry Trengrouse, a cabinet maker of Helston, who was so impressed by what he saw he set his mind to invent some way of saving shipwrecked mariners. He invented the Breeches Buoy, and in so doing, spent his life savings of £3,500, receiving in return from the Admiralty the princely pension of fifty pounds a year and a silver medal. Strangely enough, the Emperor of Russia sent him a diamond ring. I wonder where that ring is today? And who remembers Henry Trengrouse?

* * *

Here and there on this centre rib of Cornwall rise the ruined chimneys of the mines, some of them grown to the very top with ivy, the buildings roofless and desolate, and the mines themselves, fearful black chasms, are fenced around, sometimes insecurely. Perhaps it is the sight of these ruins which gives to the country a somewhat depressing effect. Even when the ivy strives to clothe the naked brick, ugliness still remains.

It was at the beginning of the eighteenth century that rich deposits of copper and tin were found in Cornwall. They were at first worked in a very primitive way. In 1777, James Watt visited the country to erect the first steam pumping engines to keep the mines free from water.

Work in these pits must have been a horrible business, if we read of the conditions of those days. Tuberculosis was rife, as were other respiratory diseases, which killed off thousands of miners.

The wretched men worked by candlelight, the candles being fixed to their caps by clay sockets, and the temperature in some of the deep mines was as much as 115°. Few miners survived to the age of fifty.

In the middle of the nineteenth century Cornwall was producing half the world's output of tin, a fact which seems hard to believe.

It was not until the first world war that the rot began. The mine owners were told to drop all development and concentrate on bringing up all the tin they could, and after the war the industry was left ruined and derelict, terrible depressions and unemployment followed, but a few mines still struggled on until 1939.

Trebarwith.——The Abandoned Mine

Then came cheap tin from the Straits Settlements. This was the final death blow. It is very doubtful if they will ever be worked again, for the task of pumping the old workings dry would be beyond the powers even of modern machinery, and in view of the cheaper foreign tin it would not be warranted. Yet, what treasure lies below those stony hills! In addition to tin, there is of course copper, and even gold.

In the early days of mining there were no mechanical aids for descending the pits. The men climbed up and down by ladders, which in itself must have been an exhausting process, even more so after a hard day's work.

123

In 1841 a man named Matthew Loam invented what was called the 'Cornish Man Engine'. This was a vertical rod which extended to the bottom of the shaft. It was wound by an engine which moved the rod twelve feet up and twelve feet down in alternate strokes. Up the shaft there were platforms, and also on the rod itself, so that the miners stepped off at intervals, all the way down to the bottom. This must have called for great sureness of foot and balance.

The mine owners at Levant installed this engine in 1850 and it was still in use in 1919; this, by the way, was the last Cornish mine to do so. In October of that year the rod snapped and twenty-one miners fell to their death.

In some cases the miners drove their galleries under the sea itself and the men, as they worked, could hear the sound of the waves above them. At Botallack mine, south of Levant, the galleries extend out to sea for a third of a mile, and are (or were) twelve hundred feet deep.

Occasionally the sea broke into these under-ocean galleries, as it did at Wheat Owles in 1892, when eighteen miners lost their lives.

The whole of the centre rib of Cornwall is dotted with these derelict workings, and one sometimes sees notices: DANGEROUS MINE WORKINGS, KEEP AWAY. Many a dog and sheep (and possibly humans too) have been lost in these fearful shafts, for they are ideal dumping places for criminals.

Perhaps it would be best if all these ruined chimneys were blown down, the buildings razed, and the old pit shafts properly and permanently protected from inquisitive wanderers. But on second thoughts, they have become so much part of the typical Cornish scene that no doubt we should miss them.

Camel Estuary

CHAPTER SIXTEEN

The Camel Country

NEXT morning we found that the hateful fog was fencing us in again. As there was no sign of it lifting we felt we could not face another day at Jim's Inn. So we set to at once and packed up our gear, paid our lodging money, waved a goodbye to the white gull who stood sentinel on the roof of the shed, and pulled away.

As we came down the hill above Penzance we saw that, as usual, when one got on the 'other side', the fog was thinning away, and soon the sun burst forth. In a moment we were back once more in the flaming heat of June, back into our old familiar weather which we had enjoyed on the golden sands of Holywell Bay.

Before us lay the unknown. That old sense of insecurity was with us again, of not knowing where we should drop anchor; we dreaded being forced on to a populous site with all its drawbacks.

By devious ways, across bare uplands where the sun blazed down with never a wayside tree to give respite, we came at last to the estuary of the Camel beyond Newquay. We left the caravan in a lay-by and went in search of an amiable farmer.

The character of the country was very different now. The little by-lanes down which we chose to travel were reminiscent of South Devon; wild privet grew abundantly in the hedgerows, scenting the heated air with its strange haunting perfume; vast waxy trusses of honeysuckle adorned the wayside bushes.

At last, as we turned down a little lane shaded with elm trees beyond the cheerful and friendly little town of Wadebridge (with a glimpse of the Camel estuary between pine woods, over which two buzzards mewed and wheeled in the afternoon sun) we found a farm site and a shady corner where tall wych elms stood to shield us from the powerful sun. There too, we found a good friend in the farmer, Mr Phillips, who was pleased to let us go down into a shady corner of his site where the shadows lay so cool, green, and inviting. Even though this was a registered caravan site, there were few vans in the field. We had the corner to ourselves.

We were expert now at dropping anchor. Winston rolled to a halt, legs were wound down, and soon we were uncoupled and the kettle was on the gas.

Tea over, we went to the bracing sands of Polzeath and very soon we were surfing in the breakers. The creamy rollers soon washed away all dust of travel, and all weariness as well, and later, we walked by honeysuckle lanes past the estuary of the Camel which glowed quietly in the evening sun.

No doubt Jim's Inn was still wrapped in chilly mist, and the white gull was sitting disconsolately on the shed in our camping field, but here all was high summer once again.

That night I awoke soon after 3 a.m. to hear the crying of the curlew packs on the estuary. Those magical sounds, heard afar off, and in the quiet of the summer dawn, brought back to me a host of memories of other days under very different conditions, of waiting for the wild geese at the break of day upon many a northern firth, of a frosty winter world of blue shadows on white snow.

At eight-thirty next morning the sides of Heron were too hot to touch for we were unshaded on our eastern side. A cirl bunting was singing in the wych elms not far away, the first I had heard on our journey. We should have heard it in Hampshire, for W. H. Hudson found that it replaced the yellow-hammer in the

Selborne district. But I had not heard a cirl there, though plenty of yellow-hammers were singing.

The oft-repeated 'zizzing' call note of the cirl has considerable carrying power. It is not unlike the sound made by some insect in the grass. With true bunting monotony and lack of originality it is repeated again and again, resembling the maddening song of the Indian coppersmith bird.

Hard by our camp a sluggish little brook wound down the valley, well shaded with trees and bushes. To it, Farmer Phillips' cows made their hasty way with upraised tails as soon as the sun climbed high. They stood flank to flank in the dark shade, swishing their anxious fly-whisks, their heads swinging ceaselessly, dreading the hum of the scouting 'gads'.

I walked a little way up this valley, keeping to the hawthorns' shade. The earth was cracked and very dry, trampled by the feet of the cattle. From the black and crusty cow pats the flies arose in a sudden hum. This valley smelt to me of the Midlands; it was hard to believe we were close to the sea.

This day, the twenty-seventh of June, was perhaps the hottest of the trip. There was no breeze to fan us under the wych elms in our sequestered corner. But such a day was not one to spend skulking in the shade. Very quickly we were away to the sea when once again I was able to try my skill with the surf board. Tired of that at last, we lay in the cool shelter of some rocks (where the sand seemed so cold to naked feet after the heated sand in full sun) and there drowsed like lazy dogs.

It is a pleasant sensation lying on a beach after a swim. The body is still refreshed and tingling, one feels absolutely at peace with the world, full of a delicious languor. With eyes closed one can hear the sounds of children shouting, the barking of dogs, people talking, the crying of gulls, and always, as a background, the low steady respiration of the sea. There are no sounds so sleep-making, so soothing, as those sounds of violent activity, going on out there on the hot sands. Even the sea cannot keep still. But you are cool and silent, life's troubles have gone for good!

Tintagel coast

CHAPTER SEVENTEEN

Port Isaac, Tintagel and Its Coves

PERHAPS the greatest attractions of the Cornish coast are the
numerous coves, caves and harbours. Let us face it, one cannot
compare the bare featureless Norfolk shoreline, with its absence of
coves, cliffs and picturesque fishing villages, with this wonderfully
varied Cornish and Devon coast. And those rock pools, full of
crystal water, full of all manner of exciting shells and fish, what
child, or adult, can resist their magic?

The Cornish coves and fishing villages seem very much of a
pattern. There is usually a fold in the high land down which flows
a little stream, its lower reaches choked with a luxuriant growth of
flag, fern and ling, and numberless bog-loving sallows.

The villages are reached only by steep and narrow lanes of one-
car width which twist and turn, designed for panniered donkeys
instead of the motor-car.

Portquin, which we visited from Wadebridge, was just such
a typical harbour. At one time it was a flourishing fishing hamlet.
It is reached by a narrow road too small, thank heaven! for
coaches and it has been able to preserve its air of privacy.

The harbour at Port Isaac

When we visited it on a boiling hot afternoon only a handful of people were bathing in the harbour which lay roasting under the sun.

The entire male population of Portquin was lost in a great gale during the last century. This tragedy inspired the famous painting by Sir Luke Fildes called 'A Hopeless Dawn', prints of which hung in many a cottage home in Edwardian days.

* * *

Another typical Cornish harbour is Port Isaac, north of Polzeath. Despite its new brash bungalows on the cliff-top, with their 'non-U' names and over-tidy gardens, the village itself, and its harbour, cannot have altered very much in the last fifty years, save that the houses now have power and light and the usual 'mod. cons.'.

Its little harbour, protected by two stone piers draped with weed, gave forth the very essence of the sea for the tide was out when we arrived and the muddy sand lay exposed to the hot sun beating down upon it. 'Working' boats, not 'play' boats, were drawn up on the edge of the amber ripples, and numberless grave, white gulls stalked about on shell-pink legs. Old jersey-clad fishermen gossiped under a wall, sitting on a rough wooden bench. Their delightful bumbling brogue was as much part of the scene as the conversation of the gulls.

I suppose that inshore fishermen are the only true hunters left in Britain. Their livelihood, despite the welfare state, depends in great measure on their skill, mixed with a certain element of luck, which no fisherman, amateur or professional, can afford to do without. During the slack tides there is nothing to do but to sit and gossip, and look at the holiday-makers. The fishermens' bread-and-butter lies out there, between those two stone piers, where one glimpses a horizontal line of indigo, flecked with white.

The natural laws of wind, weather and tide govern their comings and goings; they are almost like cormorants or other fish-eating birds. They must fish at the right time, and in the right place, and between whiles rest in the sun.

In these sunny harbours of Cornwall the hours seem to pass in slow motion. The soft bumblings of the old men mingle with the sharp strident cries of children and gulls. There is a half-rotten sweet scent in the atmosphere, a drowsy miasma which induces sleep. Look at that old fisherman on the bench below the wall. His head has slumped sideways, his peaked cap has slipped over one eye. The toothless mouth gapes slightly, and a dribble of saliva glistens in his stubble beard. Perhaps he is vaguely aware of the smells and sounds outside his body, for at such times we retire, as it were, within our outer shell, and the noises and other sensations of the world only reach us distantly, as from another room.

He hears, albeit faintly, the sudden hyena-like cry of a black-backed gull, or the chuckling laugh of another as it flies over, its purple shadow following it over the hot mud.

His aged nose brings, perhaps, the taint of decaying cods' heads down by the boats, the occasional passing whiff of cheap perfume from the holiday girls.

He sleeps as an old dog sleeps, with an occasional twitch of a limb, a jerk of a leg. Take this old man out of this environment, shut him up, say, in Birmingham or London, even put him in a local hospital, and he would die as a caged wild bird dies.

I wonder if the young men of these Cornish villages take to the sea as their fathers have before them? Surely the motor-cycle and the 'tele' rob them of their virility? One fisherman I talked to shook his head sadly and said that many of the young chaps were after more money and could only get it in the towns.

But a few, he said, could not resist the call of the sea, it was part of them, of their inner soul. They would be fishermen until the end of their days. In fullness of time these young men will come to the bench under the wall, and sleep maybe as that old man sleeps, for how can these places ever change?

Big, broad-shouldered gulls, snow-white and pearly-grey, stood about on the warm sand, looking at us under beetling brows from their pale suspicious eyes. They have shoulders like boxers, magnificent birds with never a quill out of place, so smooth of feather and form they seem to be carved out of flawless alabaster. Some sleep on one leg, the other quite invisible, tucked out of sight, but usually one eye regards you with watchful wariness. They have never wholly lost their fear of man, nor will they allow the camera-clicking tourists to take any liberties. They fly leisurely away if approached nearer than five feet.

* * *

Down near the quay at Port Isaac is a fascinating antique shop which many a visitor to this delightful little port must know. It is crammed with all those treasures which delight the male of whatever age, all the junk that seafaring men bring back from the Orient.

There are enough cutlasses to furnish a boarding party of pirates, old muskets, antique chased pistols, which always have such a fascination for me (but which I can never afford to buy), coloured shells, wonderful butterflies, and beads, woven baskets, musical instruments, flutes and pipes, pots and pans, floats, nets, old yellow maps, and I know not what else, all telling of the romance of the voyager's life, and of distant sunny lands where gaudy parrots cry harshly in the jungles, and where befeathered men shake their spears in the tribal dance.

As we walked about the little narrow streets the sun beat down with power; we were glad to keep in the blue shadows of the tall houses. It shone upon the unending rusty chains which lay sprawled across the mud, upon the hanging nets, upon the carcases of rotting dog fish which lay with their shark-like, under-shot mouths agape, poor weeds of the sea, jetsam of the hauled nets, upon the coils of glistening seaweed, under which many a crab cowered miserably, praying for the tide's order of release. There hung about the harbour that familiar smell of fish, both fresh and tainted, mixed with the faintest suggestion of sewage which is inseparable from these Cornish harbours at the foot of the cliffs. Do not think that this smell is unpleasant, far from it, it is the true bouquet of *sea*.

Some fishermen, the younger ones, who were as yet too lusty

and too full of life to sleep under the wall, were busy over their oars, rowing in leisurely fashion across the warm shallow harbour water where small boys were swimming and larking about with rubber rings. Wicker pots lay among the tangled ropes, conjuring up visions of enormous scarlet lobsters and crabs, as showy as guardsmen, the latter with arms like mechanical ore-grabbers, full of succulent white meat.

* * *

Lobster Pots
Port Isaac

Not far from the antique shop, almost opposite if I remember aright, we saw over a doorway the notice, simple and to the point, LOBSTER TEAS!

I beg of you, should you ever find yourself in Port Isaac on a summer's afternoon (not having enjoyed a good luncheon, and maybe feeling like 'a little something'), do not pass this crooked doorway!

Entering, you ascend a flight of wooden stairs flanked by binnacles, nets, floats and all the rather bogus paraphernalia we find in such eating-houses, and you will find yourself in a cool upper room with a gallery which overlooks the harbour below.

And there (after a suitable anticipatory pause) will appear

before you a lobster (or lobsters) which might grace the table of Lucullus. They recline upon a couch of crisp 'snoppy' lettuce, laced with cold, fresh cucumber slices, cut thin; they are enormous, *rosy*, fit subject for a Dutch still-life painter, and with them you will eat fresh brown bread and Cornish butter. In France you would drink wine with them, some clean sharp wine, but in Port Isaac (and being British) you will make do with hot sweet tea in thick cups. You will eat at leisure, whilst hearing through the open windows the mewing of gulls, sounds of hammering, squeals of children, barking of dogs, and those faint, far-off, intermittent knocking sounds of people 'messing about in boats'.

* * *

I have not said enough about the Cornish sea caves, for almost every cove can boast at least one. Two of the best, which can be visited without a boat, are at Tintagel and Trebarwith. At Tintagel, where I went on my usual fruitless quest of the chough, I entered Merlin's Cave, that narrow echoing cranny under King Arthur's Castle.

At low water you may enter, as I did, hopping from rock to glistening rock, to the far postern way, where the green walls of water come mounting and raging as though to sweep you away like a beetle in a pond. Their tumultous thunder echoes hollowly from the glistening cold walls, and all is wrapped in a sombre twilight.

I met an American in the shadows busy with his costly movie camera. He was trying to get a picture of the sea as it battled at the entrance, of the columns of white spray through which the brilliant light made play.

'Gee! it's sure some place,' he said. 'They tell me it's called the tripper's trap when the tide comes in. It's coming in now, brother —guess I'm quittin'.' I asked the attendant (who lurks behind the high entrance door to King Arthur's Castle) if he had ever seen a chough. Yes, he had *as a boy* long years ago, but now there was only one pair on the coast between Tintagel and Padstow.

Like many another pilgrim that boiling day I climbed the dizzy

The 'Trippers' Trap', Tintagel

heights of Castle Hill, a somewhat embarrassing but interesting ascent beneath a purposeful, dark-haired girl who had blue ribbons slotted into the hem of her crisp white petticoats. I emerged, gasping, on the toast-coloured ramparts and for company had a little blue butterfly (the dark-haired one had, to my sorrow, unaccountably vanished among the rugged walls) and there I lay full-length on the turf and looked out on the vast arc of glittering sea.

This view from Castle Hill must be unmatched in all Cornwall. As I write this I can feel again the warmth of the sun upon me, and smell the thyme and the salt winds.

The continuous procession of trippers of all ages, and of all classes, up and down the worn and precipitous paths, reminded me of egg-bearing ants. One never hears of accidents on these truly dizzy steeps, which is surprising, for quite aged people were struggling up and down with admirable British determination.

As we came down from the hill, Ping caused us some embarrassment by choosing to do her business right in the centre of the dusty path. The resulting confusion caused much merriment amongst the trippers who pressed onwards from behind, but all movement up or down was suspended until nature had taken its course, and the procession could continue once more.

Perhaps because Tintagel was so infested with people I preferred the less spectacular but more deserted Trebarwith beach, with its glorious rock pools and firm, golden sands, upon which the great waves crashed at intervals, an ideal beach for surfing.

Fulmars glided about the crests of the cliffs, and I explored the huge, impressive cave on the left of the beach, penetrating to its inmost recesses, where the tumult of the sea was but a faint echo, and the dominating sound only the hollow 'tink tonk' of moisture falling from the roof.

One dark recess was of an impenetrable blackness and the chilled air sent a shiver down my spine. It was a relief to get out again into the sunlight, and all the bustle of joyous light and warmth.

Near Hartland—

CHAPTER EIGHTEEN

The North Coast and Boscastle

As soon as the sun shone through the windows on the morning of the twenty-ninth of June I was awakened from sleep by the advent of two bluebottles. Now the arrival of a bluebottle in the confined space of a caravan can provide a lively game which is known as 'Bluebottle Ping-pong'. It requires three players (in bed) armed with fly-swatters. You would hardly believe how difficult it is to bring the target down, for a bluebottle is more agile than a snipe and infinitely harder to hit. I have often wondered if the backroom boys of aviation have studied the flight of bluebottles sufficiently.

I bagged one, a beautiful flying shot, the other fled out of the skylight. Ping, who is an active fly hunter, acted as middle stop. She has on many occasions captured a bluebottle in full flight, a feat far from easy for a dog with a blunt little mouth, and she eats them greedily.

Unfortunately, on this morning, my daughter was suffering from an overdose of lobster and was left in bed whilst Cecily and I went to Boscastle to collect our post.

We had expected to find another typical Cornish cove village and so it proved, a perfectly delightful little harbour which is reached by a tortuous passage from the open sea. The tide was coming in, rolling the fishing boats; the sun winked on the ripples and set the ships' masts gleaming. White gulls marched about and quarrelled by a little stream which comes down from the high ground. It was much as we had imagined it.

In the centre of the village close to the bridge which crosses the brook I saw a newly-emerged Tiger moth, though which of the species I could not see. It was flying about like an exotic gaudy butterfly over the bright water. Eventually it settled on a large flat stone in mid-stream. It had barely done so when a grey wagtail came dipping daintily down the brook and alighted on the same stone beside it, but ignored the brightly coloured insect. Then both flew away. I noticed quite a number of Tiger moths (which are day fliers) in and around Boscastle, so it must be quite a locality for them.

We climbed the towering cliffs on the north side of the cove until we could look down on the harbour and village spread out below. The shallow water was a pale aquamarine and the deeps, winding paths of violet and indigo. Soon we spied a tiny motor-boat far out on the blue expanse of open sea. It was making for the harbour mouth, the waves breaking white over its bows. After

what seemed a very long while, it passed through the crooked channel below us, still tipping and tossing. By the time we regained the quay it was tying up and the two fishermen began to unload their catch of gleaming mackerel, whose silky sides were shot with many rare blues, greens and silvers. I asked one of the men if he would sell us three for supper. He looked up briefly, then tossed us up three beauties.

'How much?' I enquired.

'On the house!' he said with a grin, a typical gesture of these kindly Cornish people.

Only those who have tasted mackerel fresh from the sea know just how delicious they can be, and the same applies to herring.

The post office at Boscastle is up the hill in the old part of the village and on reaching it we found it shut for the dinner-hour. So we went down again to the harbour and had some excellent chicken sandwiches and three cups of tea, which cost us only 3s. The teashop was the converted forge with the anvil still in one corner.

* * *

What a noble coastline it is from Hartland to Tintagel! From the high ground above Boscastle you see the rampart of cliffs stretching northwards, misty and blue, their bases fitfully gleaming with white surf. Somewhere down that length was *the* bird I wished to see, the Cornish chough.

What can be the reason for its rarity and its disappearance from these rugged and inaccessible cliffs? Egg collectors cannot be blamed. In actual fact, I do not think it has ever been plentiful. The jackdaws harry it and steal its nesting holes, and possibly its eggs, just as the sparrows rob the gentle house martin's. The chough's bill, slender and curved, can be no match for the jackdaw's which is like a mattock.

In *Witherby's Handbook* it says that the chough is not always confined to the coast; in some parts of Wales it haunts old slate quarries quite a long way from the sea; and may also be seen feeding with rooks and jackdaws far inland. It is resident on many of the sea cliffs in Ireland.

139

CHAPTER NINETEEN

Butterflies on the Cliff-tops

THE first of July dawned, as usual, gloriously hot. By nine-fifteen we had had breakfast and were close-coupled. We said goodbye to kind Mr Phillips, paid his modest fee and pulled out of the gate.

On his pitch we had had every consideration and convenience, milk from his cows, fresh eggs, water—everything we required.

We were gradually edging northwards now and we next dropped anchor in a remote and sequestered little meadow at a place called Middle Penline. This had been recommended to us by some fellow campers on our last pitch and a truly attractive place it proved to be. The field was full of flowers and wild thyme which smelt sweetly under our wheels as we rolled to our anchorage.

The slope of this meadow was so great that we had to block Heron's starboard wheel to get her on an even keel, but once this was done we were all set and comfortable. On our weather and sun side we had a high hedge of sallow and willow, and through a gap in the softly rounded hills could glimpse the far blue sea, with Lundy Island sitting like a cloud on the horizon.

Above us was a real summer sky across which puffy white clouds sailed in lazy fashion, dissolving away as they voyaged, like lumps of ice in water.

As a child I used to lie in the grass and watch these fine-weather clouds dissolving. One can select a small specimen and watch it as it moves majestically across the heavens and see it becoming smaller and smaller, until it melts completely into the deep blue background.

* * *

Having seen Heron safely berthed I took the Landrover and went to Crackington Haven which was not far away. I left Winston to grill in the dusty little car park and followed the National Trust path up the headland and along the edge of the cliffs, threading the slippery track between thymy banks and gorse-clad hillocks.

Crackington Haven was, at one time, one of the localities where the rare Large Blue butterfly was found, an insect I have never seen on the wing. It still occurs in North Devon and Cornwall. A friend of mine, a keen and knowledgeable entomologist, discovered a strong colony in Cornwall quite by accident a few years ago. The story is worth telling.

He happened to be motoring down one of those steep little lanes which lead to the sea when he stopped his car in a gateway. The locality seemed to have something about it which suggested it might be a likely place to find this rare species, so he climbed the gate and walked up the rough hillside. In a very few moments he saw one, and then several more, and realized he had stumbled on a strong colony. As far as I know, they still occur at that spot; my doctor friend has caught several there since, but he is not disclosing the exact locality, not even to me!

The Large Blue is an unobtrusive insect, very little bigger than the Common Blue, and has not the same rich tint of the latter. It is distinguished by the black 'darts' on its wings which no other of the 'Blues' possesses.

For a number of years entomologists were very puzzled about

the larvæ of this insect. The caterpillars were found feeding on wild thyme but for some reason they never survived in captivity. They fed normally until they were about twenty days old and then died. In May 1915, F. W. Frohawk and Dr T. A. Chapman discovered a fully-grown larva on the roots of some wild thyme at Hartland Quay. They noticed that ants were busy around it. After careful watching it was discovered that one ant takes the fully-grown larva down into the nest where the ants 'milk' it of a sweet secretion, just as they milk the greenfly aphides.

It is fed by the ants on their own larvæ, in exchange for this delicious 'honeydew'.

The Large Blue caterpillar remains in the ants' nest all winter, to emerge as a butterfly the following summer, crawling up out of the dark prison below ground into the sunlight and sweet cliff air.

How strange this is, and how, in the name of wonder, did this arrangement come about in the first place? Over many thousands of years Nature has been working out this complicated life cycle. So where ants are found amidst wild thyme on the cliffs there is always a chance of a Large Blue, but it is never found *away* from the proximity of ant colonies.

It occurs on the Cotswolds in a certain locality, which I know, and it also occurred, until the end of the nineteenth century, at Barnwell Wold in Northamptonshire. When the ground came under the plough the butterfly seemed to die out, but I often wonder if it still flies there in some odd corner where the wild thyme blooms. The Barnwell Wold race was the finest of all the Large Blue variations, being bigger and brighter.

As I followed the winding sheep track through the hot hay fields, making my way towards the mighty cliff of Cambeak, I eagerly scanned the rough hillsides for a glint of blue. But though I saw many of the common variety I never glimpsed the tell-tale black darts upon the wings.

As I drew near the summit, surrounded by mattresses of purple ling, I noticed multitudes of pretty Green Hairstreaks flying about over the tops of the herbage, the only truly green butterfly we have on the British list. With them were Burnet moths by the countless thousands, and now and again a Grayling flew by. These strange, sea-loving butterflies have wonderful powers of camouflage. When they settle they seem to snuff out like a light. Why they take so much trouble to hide themselves is puzzling. There must be some reason for it. Perhaps they have a specially nice taste for insect-eating birds. The common white butterflies never seem to bother to conceal themselves, and though I have occasionally seen them chased and taken by sparrows, they seem to be left alone by most.

There was a raven croaking hoarsely from the topmost stone of Cambeak, and when I reached the ultimate rock, I saw below what looked like the remains of his nest on a dizzy ledge.

There was a strong updrift of air against the vertical face of the cliff and about this sooty black swifts shot hither and thither, passing so close to my head I could hear the rush of their wings. On the very tip of Cambeak the air was still, for the wind was being deflected upwards over my head, as it is off the windscreen of a travelling car.

But behind me on the slopes of ling the breeze was strong enough to toss a stonechat's tail over his back as he scolded me from the top of a bush of furze.

Bees were everywhere; their murmurous hum filled the air, for that morning the sea was sleeping below the cliffs and hardly made a sound.

I steeled myself to stand on the very lip of Cambeak. I had to force myself to look down. Below—far, far below—the sea was dwarfed and crinkled: a ghastly spinning drop which turned my stomach over.

Looking northwards and westwards over the deep blue sea, all glittering and peaceful under the burning sun, it was fascinating to study the oily 'slicks' far offshore. Some were highways, many times broader than the M1, others wound this way and that like the track a moorhen leaves in a weedy pond.

These stretches of calm, these paths and oily ribbons can, I suppose, be read and understood by seafaring men, and indicate the set of the tide and the sea's mood.

143

I came back down the southern slope of Cambeak and found it
milky with a multitude of spiders' webs which were woven about
the tips of the ling-like shrouds.

Great green grasshoppers, vastly handsome creatures, sprang
away before my moving feet. These grasshoppers are miniature
jungle tigers for they prey on smaller specimens of their kind.

A beautiful little cock stonechat, so smart in his summer dress
of black, russet and white, stood on a dead branch above a bramble
thicket and swore at me. He was soon joined by his drab mate:
they must have had a nest close by. But no bird is more wary
(unless it is the greenshank and the bunting) of betraying its nest.

The stonechat's world is always that of flinty upland, sea
winds, blown furze, wild commons and hot sand. You might
think it is a typical summer visitor, but it is resident in many
coastal districts of Devon and Cornwall, though migrations do
take place.

The swifts, seeing me descending the cliff, seemed to wish to
accompany me, for they came shooting down the slope over my
head. Perhaps I was disturbing insects from the herbage. Also
with them were a few slow-flying sand martins.

I had been watching a large nesting colony of these latter birds
the evening before in a sand bluff at Damer Bay. The sun was
setting in a glorious riot of colour over the sea, and this was
reflected in the gently rippling tide which was on the turn.

Sunset Damer Bay

The martins flew back and forth, twittering sweetly. Some came from the nesting burrows with white baby droppings in their bills, which they let fall in the crinkling tide. Nearly all birds take a very great care of nest hygiene, all save the kingfisher, who, despite his glorious attire, is unspeakably dirty in his nesting habits.

Ping in bed with C

CHAPTER TWENTY

St Gennys and the Coast

IN nearly all our camps we had trees to look out upon, or thick bushes.

At Middle Penline we had sallows, the small-leaved variety (the differences between variations of the sallow are considerable). Each morning I would get out of bed and open the van door so that I could lie back and enjoy the intricate tangle of leaves, all of various shapes and sizes. Mingled with the sallow was hazel, and ash, the lower stems of which were thickly bearded with silvery lichen and muffled in ivy. In the damp ditch below grew ferns of many kinds. What interested me most were thickets of that rather rare plant, the milk parsley, which is the food plant of that regal butterfly, the Swallow-tail, whose wings are fashioned rather more for a tropical forest than for our homely little island. These delicate, graceful plants put me in mind of a day I spent a few years ago in a Norfolk fen searching for the handsome green-and-black caterpillars of this beautiful butterfly. I spent a long time searching, until Angela and Cecily discovered several nearly full-grown larvæ which we brought home and later hatched successfully.

As they feed upon the tops of the milk parsley they make no attempt at concealment, for birds will not touch them. The caterpillar of the Swallow-tail has a strange branched feathery ornament which it protrudes from its head when alarmed and which gives forth a most powerful strange aroma. As a polite warning to others it is also coloured in Nature's 'danger colours', with black-and-yellow bands.

Mingled with the milk parsley and sallow at Middle Penline were straggling water mints, rosebay willow herb and brambles. I do not know why such finely cut detail gives such pleasure to the eye. Hudson once remarked on the pleasure he had from looking at a level forest of bracken fronds.

* * *

If one has exceptionally long sight (as I have) there is always the chance of spotting the nicked and eaten leaves which betray the presence of a feeding caterpillar. It might be a Hawk moth, or even (in Midland forest country) the caterpillar of the king of all the butterflies, the Purple Emperor. One morning at Middle Penline, when I was thus lying idly on my bunk watching the insects busy among the bright leaves, I noticed that a spray of privet halfway up the hedge was being agitated in a steady gentle motion. At once I saw the outline of a magnificent Privet Hawk Moth caterpillar. It was busily feeding, its head nodding like that of a cart-horse pulling a plough. I suppose that the caterpillar of this species is one of the most striking in shape and colouring, with its apple-green sides and bold maroon-and-white diagonal lines along its flanks. It is a hefty creature when fully-grown and with an imposing horn, like that of a rhino, on its stern.

The purpose of this horn (the caterpillar of the Purple Emperor also has it) is, I am sure, a form of protection against annoying parasites. I have seen a Purple Emperor caterpillar twisting its horn violently when a greenfly crawled upon its back.

What a joyous discovery it was when one of these big brightly marked larvæ presented itself to a schoolboy's eyes! One can never forget the shock of delighted surprise when one suddenly saw one of these strange creatures upon a stem of privet. (I think all caterpillars fill the *female* mind with horror for they regard them as untouchables, akin to spiders and mice.)

We so quickly forget those days of boyish triumph and the gloating over a newly-discovered specimen—how rich those little discoveries made our world, what vast importance we attached to them!

In the last few years moth collecting has taken on a new interest for, with the new powerful lamps, 'mothing with sugar' has become a thing of the past. Now we have found that certain light rays can draw moths from great distances and many which were thought to have been rare, or even extinct, have been taken in some numbers.

Moths are not only attracted to light. The female emits a powerful smell which can attract the male. Only lately I heard from a doctor friend of mine (he who discovered the Large Blue colony) a most interesting story which shows how powerful this scent can be.

He visited the great Forest of Wyre in Worcestershire to search for the lovely rare Kentish Glory moth which is much prized by collectors. The male is smaller in size than the female and more richly coloured—tawny-red with delicious markings on the fore-wings of white, umber and black. The female is, however, the more handsome. She is twice the size of her consort and her colouring is more restrained and delicate.

It is a day flier—and a fast one to boot—so it is by no means easy to net, for it spends much of its time darting about the higher forest boughs.

My friend saw no sign of his prize all through a long spring day but he had with him a female which had been lent to him to allure the male. He left the forest in the afternoon but before doing so exposed it—in a little cage—to the air without any visible result.

He then started off and had not gone many yards down the road when he happened to glance in his driving mirror and saw that a moth was pursuing his! He stopped the car, got out, exposed the female, and netted a fine specimen of the Kentish Glory!

This moth, which is looked upon as a forest species, has, however, been taken in some abundance on Rannoch Moor in Scotland, which is a bare and desolate stretch of country with few trees.

I am certain that, with the new lamps, entomologists hardy and energetic enough to penetrate into the more lonely and less accessible corries of the Highlands would discover completely new species of moths and insects.

There was another interest for me as I lay on my bed studying the sun-warmed layers of leaves. All manner of flies were continually visiting the bushes and sidling about enjoying the sense of warmth, no doubt feasting on the honeydew upon the surfaces of the leaves. In the background among the lower growth the little whitethroats kept up a continuous bubbling song which is so much a part of the English summer hedgerow.

I was amused to read in a local guide-book which I purchased in Tintagel the list of 'rare' birds found in Cornwall. It listed whitethroat, moorhen, blackcap and raven, but never mentioned the chough!

How tiresome it is to read these blown-together guide-books, compiled by men who know nothing of their subject. Even a writer with little knowledge of natural history can easily check up on his facts with local ornithologists.

*   *   *

That evening of the second of July was perhaps the most beautiful of the trip. The sun had shone all day and towards evening the entire western sky was streaked with wisps of cirrus cloud.

We went, before the sun had set, to the little lost hamlet of Cleave, some six miles west of Boscastle.

The tiny church of St Gennys crouches in the shelter of a low hill, its short well-proportioned tower barely catching the sea winds for it is as well protected as the church at Gunwallowe.

Below is the secluded vicarage with its garden gay with flowers, surely one of the most beautiful parsonages in Britain. From its lawns you can look northwards over the heathery cliffs to the brilliant blue sea. It is the sort of place where Rupert Brooke might have lived and about which he could have written a descriptive poem.

Below the vicarage wall the ground fell steeply into a ferny coomb, at the bottom of which sparkled a bright stream. We could see Lundy clearly in the pellucid light of evening, away there on the horizon.

Young rabbits skipped playfully about the ferny slopes and the turf was burnt toast-brown and full of large deep cracks. We climbed the steep path on the opposite hill, picking our way through dense blackthorn with some difficulty, and stood at last on the ultimate ridge. We found the view rather disappointing. The shore below was a mass of tumbled grey boulders with no sand or coves.

Even the cliffs themselves, viewed at close quarters, were dour and wore a Welsh aspect.

From that high vantage point we could look down into the clear green depths and see the layers of rock leaning one upon another like books on a shelf, stretching out from the shore to gradually lose themselves in the deeper seas.

I had noticed this same formation when I visited Hartland Point the day before in search of the Large Blue. There the submarine rock is even more distinctive; the level ridges can be seen, like corrugated cardboard, stretching far out under the sea.

There was an ancient sixteenth-century box tomb in the churchyard at Cleave, a very early example, if not the earliest in the country, and on the north side were two huge box tombs, dating, I suppose, from the late eighteenth or early nineteenth century. They had both collapsed drunkenly and gaped obscenely: a ghoulish sight for little village children who came for Sunday afternoon catechism.

I could imagine them peeping fearfully in, half expecting to see some frightful sight of mouldering shrouds and grinning skulls. I was reminded of a story told to me by an aged lady who, when she was a girl, was greatly intrigued by one of these ruined old box tombs in a Midland churchyard.

One winter night she was passing through the churchyard on

her way home and saw a pale ghostly light shining within the stone box. She was, of course, terrified, and ran screaming to her parents who thought she was imagining things. But the child was obviously so horror-stricken that they summoned a constable and all three went to investigate. The light was shining, right enough, ghostly and pale through cracks in the stone. On closer investigation they found a tramp inside, with an old coat around him, a candle to read by and a hunk of bread and cheese for supper. The stone tomb formed his only shelter and he had no use for workhouses.

* * *

The gravestones in the churchyard of St Gennys are not decorated with those beautiful gold and rosy lichens which are such a feature of the Hampshire churchyards and which W. H. Hudson found so entrancing.

The church is beautifully kept, as are the vicarage grounds, with their well-tended flower-beds and neatly mown lawn. I could imagine a white-haired Gilbert White type of cleric living there, and indeed there must be much to write about on that wild and lovely coastline.

I so fell in love with Cleave I went again by myself the next morning, which was a Sunday.

No bells rang out over the quiet cliffs and sea. I fear this was a sign of the times and the slow decay of religious observances. I will not say of *belief*, for I am sure that, despite this 'brave new world' man is still concerned as to what will happen to him after death, just as he knows by instinct what is evil and what is good.

I, for one, do not regret the passing of the bells. They have a melancholy Puritanical sound. Near at hand they are harsh, like the sound of bagpipes, but from a distance they have—again like the bagpipes—considerable enchantment, albeit (for me) a touch of melancholy.

In the churchyard, beyond the ruined box tombs, I came upon three pathetic graves. Two were of English boys, one lost in 1914, the other in the last war, and between them was the grave of a

151

German airman, OGEF F. PRIMKE, who was killed on Christmas Eve, 1941. Seeing these graves of three young men cut off in the prime of life made me full of sad thoughts. By rights they should still be in the world with me, enjoying this peerless summer morning, but because of wrong-headed thinking on the part of politicians and a few evil men, one a madman, their lives had been snuffed out. Who, in heaven's name, ever gave them a thought now? And what strange grim fate ordained that this German boy should have perished so far from his homeland on Christmas Eve—his broken body to lie in a remote Cornish churchyard without even a flower upon his resting-place?

I came out from the sight of those churchyard graves full of melancholy. I was glad to be greeted by a merry cock wheatear who perched on an ant hill and shook his tail at me, his breast the tint of sunlight reflected from hot sand.

At the very end of the cliff a buzzard soared and mewed, and upon the hot heathery slopes numberless goldfinches, linnets and other finches were busily feeding on the seeded heads of grasses and weeds.

I sat upon a cliff-top hummock and watched them through my powerful binoculars until the sun became so unbearably hot I descended into the valley, glissading down the slippery turf and dodging the boulders. There I came upon a deep and crystal stream which came meandering down the valley in true Cornish fashion to spill over the cliff-edge in a whispering veil and fall, ultimately, directly into the deep sea under.

I followed up its course with the sweat pouring from me until I came upon an enchanting pool fringed with loosestrife and fern, a narrow oblong pool with floor and sides of clean-washed granite. The water appeared no more than three feet deep but when I stripped off shirt and shorts and stepped in I was up to my neck in two strides.

A stroke or so and I was at the throat of the pool where the stream came gushing with a merry noise between two slabs of granite.

Never have I enjoyed a swim more! After a sea bathe one is

refreshed but the body is sticky with salt. The pure hill-water washes you clean, as clean as it washes and varnishes the coloured pebbles. I rolled and splashed like a joyous seal, watching above me the slow gyrations of the buzzard and busy transparent gulls passing high over against the vivid cloudless blue, and the bees, working the flowers of the rosebay willow herb, and bands of twittering linnets which kept shuttling to and fro across the valley where they continued to feed on the roasting hillside opposite.

A little higher up the stream, where an alder grove formed a little swampy thicket, the chiff-chaffs were still in full song and what bird indeed could *not* sing on such a morning! Indeed, I sang myself, at the top of my voice, and only the gulls made answer.

* * *

It was from this camp at Middle Penline that we visited the delightful town of Bideford. Despite the crowds of visitors, which even in June were considerable, there was an old-world air about the place. The quay was musical with gulls and fishing boats were tied to the walls, with red-brown nets hung to dry on the rigging. Across the vivid blue waters the green fields and woods shook in the heat and jersey-clad fishermen slept in the sun.

CHAPTER TWENTY-ONE

Mumper's Dingle

W E awoke on the morning of the fourth of July to rain and heavy clouds which trailed their skirts raggedly across the distant valley. It seemed quite strange to have no sun and no blue sky. The air was full of those sweet nameless perfumes which come after weeks of drought. This rain was to be the onset of the long wet spell which was such a feature of late 1960.

The sight of these overcast skies decided us. We would 'jall' onwards into Somerset, keeping to the by-lanes as far as we could. Even as we wound up the legs of Heron and made a last inspection of the gear the light grew brighter.

The night's rain had made our thymy meadow slippery; I had to engage Winston's lower gear to pull us up the slope. We followed the Bideford road to Stratton, and there left the coastal road and made towards Holsworthy. Just beyond South Molton we took a turning marked UNFIT FOR CARAVANS AND HEAVY TRAFFIC.

We had been through so many rough places and steep and narrow lanes that we greeted this notice with derision—nothing

could be worse than those lanes about the Dart! But we were soon
to be sobered up.

By now the sun was out once more with all its old power and
we were soon feeling both hungry and weary, and extremely
thirsty. And now, sure enough, the road began to deteriorate.

We stopped at a little wayside tavern, neat and clean, where
I had a glass of rare mild ale on the recommendation of mine host.
He and his wife were artistic, intelligent people, ex-Navy, and
they told me they had only been there six months.

The place was spotless and the mild ale of great excellence and
as I drank we talked of many things. On the walls of the smoke-
room I noticed two fine oil paintings, one of Windsor Castle from
the river, another of Eton College on an autumn evening. They
were painted in masterly fashion and I learnt that the landlord's
father had done them, and was an artist by profession.

I could have stayed there a long while but we had to push on,
for I now planned to camp somewhere on Exmoor by sunset.

It did not take us long to realize that what the warning notice
said was true, the road was indeed unfit for vans, or even motor-
cars! We dived up and down the most appalling hills and two cars
we met practically ditched themselves to let us by.

Gradually we got away on to higher ground and at last reached
the bleak moor itself. Bare and barren pastures and no trees
anywhere gave us a chilly feeling down our spines, especially now
that we had lost the sun for good and the wind was moaning in
the side curtains of Winston with a wintry pipe which boded ill.

We were tired too, and a little on edge, due no doubt to the
fearful switchback road we had chosen to take us to the moor.
We could see no place where we wanted to halt. The farms crouched
behind their few ragged trees like ill-tempered terriers. I saw no
streams, dells, nor coombs, until, diving down off the high ground,
we came on a bright river and a sharp bend and trees in a tangle.

By a stone bridge I glimpsed a little opening, a sort of ferny
dingle, grown up with all manner of wild growth and bushes. In
a moment I had swung the squat nose of Winston inwards and we
pulled into Mumper's Dingle. We had some difficulty in turning

the van round by hand for the way was narrow, though we had a hard bottom. Within a few inches of Heron's wheel the ground fell steeply to a brook which tumbled over mossy stones. I thought for one moment the van was going to slide backwards but Angela thrust a timely billet under the wheel and so forestalled disaster.

In a few minutes we had the tea brewing and were all set—barring accidents, such as irate landowners, keepers and grumpy farmers—for a quiet night. Five ravens were circling and cronking over the tip of a dark fir wood just above our dingle and they seemed to be having some difference of opinion with some carrion crows. Tea over, Cecily and I walked down the road to the little stone bridge and saw the merry brown Barle glinting below us through a forest of dock and willow herb. A grey wagtail was flirting with the stream, and tiny troutlings fled this way and that.

Under the eaves of two empty cottages along the lane there was a large house-martin colony, quite the largest I had seen since I was a boy. I counted no less than nineteen nests. They were all built close together, almost touching, and many little white-throated babies peered out, chittering eagerly to the adult birds which passed to and fro in continual motion below the eaves.

Simonsbath is in the centre of the Exmoor hunt; indeed it might be said to be the very centre of the moor. The bosky wood-lands and coombs about us no doubt harboured many a shy red deer but we were not to see one.

As I made my way down the steep hill, picking my course upon the stony path that wound between the coarse moor grass, I spied something white amongst the brambles by the stream. It was a solitary sheep which had made for itself a couch there. To my inexperienced eye it seemed lively enough for it stood up and stamped a foot when I drew near. Usually sheep alone like this are ailing and so was this one. I bade it goodnight (it was to be its very last night in this world) and thankfully reached the warmth and light of the van, for the haunted wood and the lone sheep had somehow depressed me. Later, as we lay in bed, we could hear the Scotch firs on the bank above the dingle soughing as they laboured under the thrust of a westerly gale which was coming straight off the top of the moor. I was glad we were on a stone 'bottom' for soon the rain began its musketry rattle once more. When we awoke next morning the sky was still full of rain.

As we breakfasted a shepherd went past the van window heading for the hill. He had a staff in his hand and a dog at his heel.

I wished him to know of the solitary sheep but by the time I had reached the door the driving rain had hidden his form from view as he toiled upwards towards the haunted wood.

* * *

The quarry close beside us must have lain derelict for many years for it was choked with sallow and huge ferns as large as the rare royal fern.

The wind and rain died at dusk and the atmosphere became stiflingly close. In the still air the midges danced their fairy fountains, and white moths appeared over the grass tips. This curious dance of the ghost moth is part of their mating ceremony but it was short-lived; as soon as darkness came they vanished.

The tiny stream below us provided us with sweet water and it contained trout, but not large enough to catch—more's the pity, as I fancied a trout for breakfast. But this was not the free Highland country where one can catch brown trout as you pluck blackberries in an English lane with none to say you nay. I was tempted to poach the Barle, but refrained from doing so, partly because the van was so cosy in our dingle and more rain was on the way.

Instead, I walked up to the fir wood. Many of the trees were stout-boled sycamores, slightly dwarfed, and with pale, blotched bark. Carrion crows cawed harshly at me as I walked up this haunted wood and a chill and ugly little wind rustled in sinister fashion in the thick leaves overhead. I found this spinney (for it was no more) petered out on the high moor and the dying light in the western sky shone eerily through the thick, close-crowding boles. I found a badgers' sett under one of the sycamores and it had been freshly used for pug marks were printed in the red earth of their front door. I sat down behind a tree in the hope they would emerge but the night was too cheerless, both for them and for me.

Black Jack

CHAPTER TWENTY-TWO

Simonsbath, Exmoor and the North Devon Coast

A GLEAMING sun around midday tempted us out of the van. The air smelt like that of a greenhouse, full of moist heat and scents of growing lush herbage. The still air of the dingle was ⁓misted with dancing gnats.

We unhitched Winston and went to see Lynton and Lynmouth, nine miles away, taking the road over the tops of the moors. This part of Exmoor is wilder and unfenced, reminding me forcibly of the Pennines. There is that same wild moorland tang in the air, the same faint crying of moorfowl.

We found Lynmouth swarming with tourists, and this despite its being the early part of the season and the weather inclement.

It was difficult to get a drink at a bar for the pubs were full to the doors. The shopkeepers were doing a roaring business, and were, I thought, singularly good-tempered when dealing with the clamorous throngs. We had to pay a shilling to park the Landrover for just ten minutes which annoyed me. 'Parking Sharks' are becoming a menace around our coasts. One wonders in many cases what legal right is enjoyed for charging parking fees on, say,

158

Lynton and Lynmouth

dunes or sands close to the beach. In several instances in Devon and Cornwall I noticed that shore-side garages had fenced off the sands and dunes and installed pay-boxes. It is surely time this racket was looked into.

Travelling down to Lynmouth through the spectacular gorge which acts as a main gutter for the moors above, it was not difficult to see how the disastrous floods overwhelmed the little village on the beach below.

The wooded hills around, the lovely wild gorge, are in themselves a great attraction, but the foreshore at Lynmouth is boulder-strewn and dreary and unsuitable for bathing. There is sadly lacking that essence of true sea.

The cliff railway from Lynmouth up to Lynton is, in itself, a draw for tourists, for it is as exciting as dodgem cars at a fair. It is certainly an ingenious contrivance. It was built in 1890 and the two cars which carry passengers are equidistant on a wire cable and are equipped with triangular-shaped tanks. The cars are set in motion by the simple and ingenious method of filling the tank of one and emptying the other, and the empty car is pulled up by force of gravity. Strict precautions are taken against a cable parting, and if this should occur automatic brakes would grip the rails.

The cars themselves wore an antiquated air and were of a decidedly Victorian aspect. It was slightly incongruous to see men and girls in shirts and shorts, and pretty summer frocks, crowding into the ornate cars. Balloon sleeves, high stiff collars and striped blazers, would have been more in keeping.

We visited the town of Dunster, and were enchanted by the bold hills clothed in woods, splashed with violet shadow, for the sun shone suddenly and the sky was a vivid blue over the hilltops.

On our return we scorned the toll road at Porlock and whizzed up Porlock Hill in Winston, passing two motors which had failed to make the climb and lay askew, with radiators boiling. Once at the top of the high moor we looked across the grey, wind-whipped sea to the Pembrokeshire coast, where the sun was shining magically, lighting up the little fields and farms.

It is down these cliffs the hunted deer often run, choosing death in the sea to death at bay among the coombs.

In Dunster I had noticed many stags' horns nailed to doorways. On one garage building at the end of the village was an exceptionally large head which I could not believe ever came from an Exmoor stag. But some fine heads do occur, worthy to be set alongside those which come from Thetford Forest.

When I walked again up to the wood that evening, which was still gloomy and with lowering clouds, I went to see if the shepherd had found the sick sheep. Apparently he had not for it lay motionless among the brambles and the rain fell softly on its sightless eyes. I seemed to see in them a mute reproach against those mysterious forces which govern everything that lives, ordaining which creature shall die young and which shall live out its span.

It is perhaps the apparent absence of compassion and 'control' which strikes like a cold dagger to the heart. We see the operation of laws which are exact and mechanical, those same laws which set the courses of the stars, and our own whirling world. Anyone who has made a long sea voyage without human company has sensed in the awful pitiless wastes of water something which seems to deny the existence of any guiding Authority. Yet during the war we know of many airmen and sailors down 'in the drink' who have had the reverse experiences, and when they have asked for deliverance it has been forthcoming in a way which seemed very like a miracle.

Next morning I heard the hoarse croakings of the ravens up in the haunted wood and no doubt they had found the carcass for they are Nature's undertakers.

* * *

There was no doubt at all now that the weather had broken, for the rain beat a deafening tattoo upon Heron's roof which made us feel we were imprisoned in a biscuit tin. Caravanning is not all unalloyed joy!

The only person in the dingle who was cheerful was a brown wren whose song seemed to send a shiver through the fern.

These Somerset wrens had quite a different song to those we find in the Midlands, and indeed they differed from the Cornish wrens. This is the only bird I know whose song pattern changes with its particular part of the country.

The heavy rain and low bruise-coloured clouds which were now ceaselessly trailing over us from the moor brought the house martins from the ruined cottages on the road to hawk about our dingle. They wheeled back and forth close over the van roof, twittering excitedly.

One afternoon I went alone up the lovely valley of the Barle which led me up into the hills. A strong wind was blowing and though the rain had ceased, only fitful gleams of sun came to cheer me. Soon I found myself in a wild and rugged coomb and might well have imagined I was in a Highland glen. On the wind came the plaintive bleat of sheep and that tangy mossy smell which one associates with the moors. I soon found myself in a most unusual wood which consisted mostly of pines growing on a steep slope. But here and there were cedars and dense bushes of yellow broom which tufted massive lichen-covered rocks. These jutted from the hillside forming miniature cliffs and precipices giving the impression of a finely planned rock garden on a gigantic scale.

It was a place where surely fairies dwelt. Can there not be as many 'little people' in North Devon as there are in Caithness ?

A buzzard was wheeling and mewing not far away and I began to search the tops of the pines close at hand for its nest. I soon saw it, built in the top of a pine. It was an enormous affair, as big round as a fair-sized table-top. The ground sloped so steeply I was able to get above the nesting tree and with my glasses I could see into the interior of the nest itself. Two fully-fledged youngsters were sitting upright in the middle of it with baby wool blowing on their heads and backs. A half-eaten rabbit lay upon the nest's rim.

No doubt this was an ancient site for I noticed the lower twigs in the foundation of the mass of sticks were green and rotten with age but those on the rim were new. It was amazing that such a

On the Dunster road

large and heavy mass could have withstood the fierce gales of winter which must, at times, funnel down this coomb. But the pine was a sturdy tree and would not have much of a 'whip' in a strong wind, so the buzzard's home was secure.

I looked eagerly for any signs of deer up these coombs for they seemed to me to form good harbours, but perhaps there was not enough woodland.

Laurence Meynell, who has written what I consider to be by far the best book on Exmoor[1] and has caught, in a remarkable way, the spirit of this wild and lovely country, tells of a deer which was found at Bairley Bridge and was killed at Exford, a point of thirty-five miles, if that is the right expression when talking of hunting the deer with hounds.

Often the hunted animal leaves the moor and takes to the sea in one last desperate effort to shake off its pursuers. When this occurs the poor beast is pursued by a motor-boat and it is incidents such as this which give a handle to the anti-blood-sport fraternity. Certainly it seems to me to savour of the unsporting to take a boat after a swimming stag. Having won the sea it should be left alone. I have heard it said that once a stag takes to the sea it will not turn back and will be drowned; this is pure wishful thinking—I have known of two cases of stags taking to the water and landing farther along the coast.

Hunting the wild deer of Exmoor is a much more complicated procedure than many people imagine. First a warrantable stag must be located by the harbourer, a man who knows the habits of the deer and has an intimate knowledge of the coombs and woods. The stag being found, the tufters are laid on, the old experienced hounds who know how to get their quarry away from the hinds. The main pack is laid on afterwards.

Though the chances of a stag making its escape from hounds are considerably less than those of the fox, it stands more chance than the otter, which, if found in a brook, is surely doomed. The hounds do not pull their victim down but bring it to bay and they soon learn to be careful of the horns which may inflict a death

[1] *Exmoor*, 1959, Robert Hale.

blow. Up to comparatively recent times the stag's throat was cut by the huntsman, a particularly beastly business; now, a humane killer is used. I have never done any stag hunting so cannot pass judgment on it. I feel myself it would be better for experienced sportsmen to shoot them (as they do in the Highlands) when they become too numerous. At the same time it is an ancient sport which matches the country well and I do not believe the sufferings of the animal can be very great now that a humane killer is used.

Nobody denies that deer do considerable damage to farmers' crops and must be kept in check by either shooting or hunting.

Not all deer who reach the coast are taken. In 1921 a big stag was found on Draydon Farm a little before four o'clock and the hunt ended on the foreshore at Culbone in moonlight. One of the huntsmen managed to get down the cliff where he found a dead hound. The stag breasted the waves with two other lion-hearted hounds in pursuit but the latter turned back; the stag went on and was lost to sight.

The most notable run ever, in the annals of the hunt, must be the Glenthorne run which took place in 1899. A fine stag was viewed at Three Waters at one o'clock and the hunt finished at the sea cliffs at Glenthorne, sixteen miles in a straight line. The stag leapt over the cliff with a famous hound, Guardsman, after him. Both were killed on the rocks below.

Rocks at Zennor —

Ping in bed

CHAPTER TWENTY-THREE

Pinkery Pond

IF you look at any large-scale map of Somerset you will see marked upon it, on the wild moor above Simonsbath, a small blue circle, and beside it are the words *Pinkery Pond*.

Now Pinkery Pond is to Exmoor what Dozemary Pool is to Bodmin Moor, or Cranmere Pool to Dartmoor. You may reach Dozemary Pool by motor coach (almost) these days, and Cranmere Pool can be safely discovered if you have a good map. But Pinkery Pond seems to be much more inaccessible.

Perhaps all open sheets of water set in wild spacious moorland, far from human habitation and without surrounding woods, are at once mysterious. Those pale, lone lochans one glimpses upon Rannoch Moor have a certain quality, but they are so numerous they tend to lose their mystery, unlike the single isolated pools and ponds where few men wander. They lie at peace, it seems, wrapped up in themselves, reflecting the summer and winter skies with equanimity. The curlew haunts them, and the heron, and in the autumn days the greenshanks flute their wild whistles about their reedy margins.

I do not know whether I ever imagined I could reach Pinkery Pond for I had heard that the only route which was safe and direct was barred by a farmer. The other route threaded the most dangerous bogs in the whole of the moor, the sinister Chains in which the hapless Carver Doone sank to his doom. But at least there was no harm in trying, and our Mumper's Dingle was as good a place as any to start from.

I began by following the upper reaches of the Barle, so as to make my expedition of greater interest, and my way took me by the buzzard's nest and the strange hanging wood of fir. Red Devon cattle, as big, it seemed, as elephants, grazed on the steep slopes of the coombs, knee-deep in bracken. I kept my glass upon them to examine their anatomy for I have had experience of disgruntled bulls in open country. To be so confronted in a treeless land is not a pleasant prospect, even if you are fleet of foot.

After following the infant Barle, which soon became narrow enough to jump in places, and after crossing the main road, I found myself in a wild part of the moor. The visibility was bad for it had begun to rain, and my map, which was soon sodden from my frequent references to it, was of no further help. After some aimless wandering I emerged on a flat and dreary tableland with tussocks of grass and bright green moss. These tussocks gurgled at times and gave a shudder when I placed a foot upon them. I had immediate visions of the despairing claws of Carver Doone uplifted to the sky as he sank from human view in the fearful black mire of the Chains. Perhaps I was foolish to go on but I knew Pinkery Pond must be near so I kept going, sometimes coming to welcome grass and ling and scattered rocks.

A new anxiety was a fine dense wetting rain which came sweeping from the south-west, just when I had caught a distant glimpse of what, I am sure, was the pond itself, set in a hollow of the naked moor, a pale dish infinitely remote and alone. But a moment later it was blotted from view by the drifting rain.

The tussocks about me were massive. They appeared to be fine, tough, reassuring footholds, cheerfully substantial. They were deceptive in an ugly way. As I jumped from one to another

167

I felt that indescribable shudder underfoot, as if I was jumping on a trampoline.

I realized it was nothing short of recklessness to go on for I have had some experience of Irish bogs and treat them with great respect, as I do bulls. It seemed only too clear to me that I was getting very close to the Chains, if I was not already amongst them. So I turned about with a feeling which hinted at panic, for my one desire now was to feel beneath me the reassuring foundations of a good hard metal road! Once my foot broke through the moss into black mire and I quickly followed back my spoor (not easy for anyone unversed in the ways of the wild) and it took me twenty minutes to regain the firmer ground. Luckily, too, at that moment, the rain began to show signs of clearing and the sun cheered me on my way back to the road. So I never *did* reach Pinkery Pond, and time did not allow me to make a further effort. But I must do so again one day.

Pinkery Pond is an artificial water with a somewhat obscure history. Apparently, it was constructed by a man named Knight in the nineteenth century. Knight was a sort of take-over-bid merchant with plenty of money behind him. He gave £50,000 for 10,262 acres in and around Simonsbath, and went on to invest a further thousand or so in the mineral rights and freehold of several farms in the neighbourhood. He also built the now famous hunting inn in the village.

His exact purpose in making Pinkery Pond is rather puzzling. Some say he had planned a fantastic waterway across the moor so as to transport ore. When he died in 1850 some mining companies thought of moving in, but nothing came of it, and the moor beat them, which is probably just as well for the country might have been spoilt. It may even be that Pinkery Pond is merely a flooded mine working, but artificial or no, it possesses mystery, protected as it is by its formidable outwork of bogs.

Maybe it holds fabulous trout but I have never heard of anyone who has fished there.

I was not sorry to regain the road and was soon descending to Mumper's Dingle where a renewed and heavy rain was falling.

I wonder, by the way, who 'Simon' was, and why he took a bath just down the road from our camp? Perhaps he was an outlaw or some noble baron. Who he was and when he lived is lost in the mists of time. Leyland, that indefatigable sixteenth-century geographer, who seemed able to get around Britain as easily as if he had owned a helicopter, describes Simonsbath thus:

'There rinnith at this place caulled Simonsbath a ryver set 'twixt two great moorish hills in a depe botom and there is a bridge of wode over the water.'

There is a bridge there still, but now it is of stone, and I doubt whether it is a very ancient one. But the brown waters still flow as they did in Simon's time, and the spotted trout rise on summer evenings and curlew call over the 'moorish hills'.

wiltshire downland —

CHAPTER TWENTY-FOUR

Full Circle

HOW near we were to completing our Cornish journey was
brought home forcibly to us when we were exploring that
forgotten part of Somerset which is known as the Brendon Hills,
a locality which suffered greatly in the disastrous floods in the
autumn of 1960.

Somewhere beyond Exford we were startled to see on the far
eastern horizon the slim pencil of the Wellington monument.
This we knew was within a mile or so of our good friend Mr Trim.
How strange to think we had wandered so far into the golden
country, to return once more almost to the identical green heart
of Somerset!

We found the comparatively small area of the Brendon Hills a
sort of no-man's-land. The hedges were composed almost entirely
of beech, which must necessitate considerable work to keep it in
check. The impression is that behind each well-trimmed wall of
green lie spacious estates and big houses, but in fact only rolling
fields are on the other side. There is no populous countryside as
suggested by these rich hedgerows. Indeed I had some difficulty

in finding a wayside pub for a midday drink. When I did so it was a squalid ale-house with sour beer, and I was served by a slatternly woman in carpet slippers with children clinging to her skirts.

But this is a peaceful land with no sounds of trains, or even planes, only the soft, muted tinkling of streams and the songs of birds, a land where summer must pass with leisured tread among the woody dells.

Its hills and vales are full of ghosts. Laurence Meynell tells of a farmer, riding his horse one night over the Brendon Hills, who saw before him a shrouded figure. His horse shied and refused to move. He was a brave man. He dismounted and went to investigate and found that what he saw was nothing but a reflection of trees in the waters of a puddle.

All the stories we have heard of 'black dogs' and other monsters about the miry country roads of Britain may be explained by these reflections.

Once, when I was walking along a country road at night, I felt the short hairs at the nape of my neck creep like the comb on a dog's back. For beside me, trotting noiselessly along at my side, was a gaunt black dog of medieval aspect. Overcoming the instant desire to panic, I took a hold of myself and saw that the dog was nothing but the inky shadows of the hanging trees which met overhead.

* * *

During our last night in Mumper's Dingle the rain beat an insistent tattoo on the roof of Heron. The noise was at times quite deafening, like the rattle of musketry, and awoke me at intervals from an uneasy sleep. At dawn, however, the storms had blown away for a space, and the sun shone brightly. As we were having breakfast I watched a meadow pipit which had its nest somewhere in the thick herbage over the brook, sitting on its favourite look-out post on a rail with its beak full of insects done up in a neat bundle. This little bird had maddened me ever since we arrived in the dingle by her secretive ways. Try as I might, I could never locate her nest, and she kept her secret to the last.

By nine-thirty we were ready and packed. We bade a fond fare-well to our snug little corner between the 'moorish hills'. It had served us well and given us shelter and peace.

As we passed the empty cottages along the lane we also waved goodbye to the house-martin colony. Many a little white chin was visible as the youngsters watched us pass below.

Somewhere beyond Exford the sun suddenly burst out from behind dark storm clouds and set the road before us steaming.

Cecily, who was driving, suddenly exclaimed 'Goodness!—look at that tortoise!'

Winston ground to a halt. Marching along the gutter was a large tortoise, evidently a wanderer like ourselves, and, like us, he carried his rooftree with him. This strange meeting instantly reminded me of the travelling hedgehog we found on the road near Bonar Bridge, when two years before we made a similar caravan journey to the Western Highlands of Scotland.

So the pilgrim was speedily on board and travelling, meteor-like, through space. It did not approve of this method of transit however and managed to misbehave down my trouser leg. So it got its own back in more senses than one. Its presence maddened Ping who growled and grumbled all the rest of the day.

Ultimately we brought it home and let it free in the garden, where it may still be, unless it decided to continue its travels, perhaps with some vague hope of one day reaching a promised land where the sand was ever warm and other tortoises would keep it company.

We had planned to make our last two camps in that strange and haunted country of Sedgemoor, about which Llewellyn Powys wrote with such beauty, and where the legends of King Arthur linger as they do about the crags of Tintagel.

But alas! as we cruised onwards through Somerset, past the endless hedges of clipped beech, the sky grew black about us once more and the ringing hills were sheeted with rain.

To add to our melancholy, as we rounded a sharp corner near Glastonbury, a milk lorry, cutting the corner fine, struck the rear of Heron, not damaging the panel in any way, but neatly removing

The White Horse of Westbury

a clip which held the door. The impact was so slight we were hardly aware of it, and only found the damage that evening when we made camp. It was ironical that we should have traversed the narrow lanes beside the Dart and suffered no damage and had at last been 'touched' on a wide, open main road.

We could see no future in dropping anchor in the melancholy rain-sodden fenlands of Sedgemoor, which, in fine weather, are such happy hunting grounds for the botanist and naturalist, for the drains are full of rare aquatics and that elusive bird the marsh warbler still nests in the dense beds of osier.

I would have liked to talk with the old basket-makers as they wove their red willows, and perhaps catch the olive-sided tench in the reedy drains. But the rain had soured us and we turned eastwards for Wiltshire and the downs. With the rain chasing us all the way to the White Horse of Westbury we thought of Savernake and our unfrequented glade.

So thither we sped, with the rain streaming down Winston's screen and the tops of the grey-green downs cloaked with mist.

We dropped anchor in our dear familiar glade at 4 p.m. on the seventh of July with a sense of relief. And how different now was the forest! No songs of nightingales to welcome us, no flowering may. Only the rosebay willow herb gave colour, and the robin trilled his autumn-sounding roundelay from the thickets of briar. I noticed the beeches had recovered from their fire blight of June. As evening fell softly damp and misty and the sky turned rose and gold over the town of Marlborough, a blackbird came and warbled for us as lustily as if it were May, and the woodpigeons cooed up in the tall beech crowns.

The sun sank, red and large, suggesting (quite falsely) a fine day on the morrow. Perhaps way back behind us the rain was still falling on Mumper's Dingle and on the body of the dead sheep beside the haunted wood. The dingle would be vacant, only the wheel marks of our outfit would be traced in the mire. In each and every little mud house the martins would be shutting their eyes in sleep, and the merry brown Barle would be gushing under the bridge.

Savernake

With this last camp in Savernake's glade our Summer Road had come full circle and this is where I, too, will bring it to an end. In six weeks' travelling we had only had, at most, five inclement days. We had skimmed the cream of summer and had, in the process, travelled 2,464 miles. Winston had consumed 132 gallons of petrol yet our total bill was no more than what one would spend on a lavish cocktail party for forty people. But what are figures?

I only know that in the succeeding weeks, when the sun had grown pale with winter, I was to think again and again of a sea so blue as to be unbelievable; of white sands upon which the creamy rollers broke in cool thunder; of that glimpse at twilight of a shy roe in the heart of a Dorset wood; and, most vivid of all, that grim castle by the sea where the wild badgers live out their uneventful but joyous lives, remote and free.

So you see, in a sense, my Summer Road to 'the end of all the land' never really ended in the green peace of Savernake on that wet July evening. I travel it in spirit still.

The trees are bare as I write these final words, the darkness of midwinter covers the earth. But the lanes of Britain are waiting. They are there, ready for me. God willing, I will surely travel them again!